ge.

FAMILY BUSINESSES:
PLANNING THE HANDOVER

6/47

FAMILY BUSINESSES:
PLANNING THE HANDOVER

by

Stewart Clark, C.A.
Partner in Charge, Family Business Department,
BDO Stoy Hayward, Chartered Accountants, Glasgow

W. GREEN/Sweet & Maxwell
EDINBURGH
1998

Published in 1998 by W. Green & Son Limited
21 Alva Street
Edinburgh EH2 4PS

Typeset by Trinity Typesetting, Edinburgh

Printed and bound in Great Britain by
Redwood Books, Trowbridge, Wiltshire

No natural forests were destroyed to make this product.
Only farmed timber was used and replanted.

A CIP catalogue record of this book is available from the
British Library.

ISBN 0414 01217 8

© The Institute of Chartered Accountants in Scotland 1998

PREFACE

Family businesses form a key part of the economy of all developed countries and represent somewhere between 70 and 99 per cent of all businesses in these countries. They do, however, have considerable problems which are not evident in non-family businesses. These are not restricted to family businesses in any one country but are common to them worldwide.

It is however only recently in the United Kingdom that family businesses are beginning to be recognised as a separate sector which is most surprising as they represent somewhere in the region of 76 per cent of all businesses. Much of this awareness is as a result of work carried out in Glasgow at the Centre for Family Enterprise by its director, Barbara Dunn and her team and by the Stoy Centre for Family Business in England.

It is through my association with these bodies that my interest in the problems of family businesses has developed and this has led to the production of this book. I hope it will fill a gap in the market as most literature presently available in the United Kingdom on the subject is USA based.

I have attempted to increase the awareness of the problems peculiar to family businesses and put forward some practical solutions to these problems. Hopefully this will result in an increase in the survival rate of the estimated 50 per cent of family businesses which will change hands in Scotland within the next 10 years. If so, I shall be well satisfied.

My sincere thanks and acknowledgement are due to Kenneth McCracken of Wright Johnston & Mackenzie, Robin McGregor of British Linen Bank and Sandy Knox my partner, for their major contributions to the chapters on The Family Constitution, Banking and the Family Business and The Fiscal Dimension respectively. I would also like to acknowledge and thank Barbara Dunn who has adapted so well the case study which she, Kenneth McCracken, Sandy Knox and I wrote and have used many times in training sessions over the last two years. I am also grateful to her for producing the genograms which are so illustrative. My thanks also go to Anne Bryce of the Institute of Chartered Accountants of Scotland for her help and guidance and finally but not least I should like to thank my secretary Janice McInnes for her patience and forbearance as she has typed and amended the manuscript many, many times over the last year.

Stewart Clark, C.A.
BDO Stoy Hayward
GLASGOW, 1998

CONTENTS

Chapter 1

INTRODUCTION

What is a family business?

There are many varied definitions of a family business but   **1.1**
one which appears to be most appropriate and is generally
accepted is that a family business is one where at least one of
the following criteria applies:

    (a) a significant number of voting shares are owned
         by a single family;
    (b) a single family group effectively controls the
         business;
    (c) a significant proportion of the business' senior
         management is drawn from the same family;
    (d) the family considers the business to be a family
         business.

It is often assumed that family businesses are small or at most   **1.2**
medium sized. Although this is true in the great majority of
cases, there are some very large family companies. In the
United Kingdom, for example, Cadbury Schweppes and
Clark Shoes are regarded as family businesses.

What is true is that the percentage of businesses which are   **1.3**
family owned increases in rural areas. This will not come as
a surprise. Most farms will be family businesses and indeed
it is usual for most businesses, *e.g.* shops, tradesmen, hotels,
etc. in rural areas to be run by families as most of the
businesses are relatively small.

1.4 It may be of interest to note that in a recent survey of family businesses in Central Scotland[1] respondents fell into the following sectors:

  (a) service sector—44%
  (b) manufacturing sector—23%
  (c) retail sector—24%
  (d) wholesale sector—9%.

These statistics confirm the view that family businesses tend to be found in sectors where the owner-manager aspect is important, such as service industries. Most local hotels, for example, are still family owned as are haulage businesses.

How important are family businesses in the United Kingdom economy?

1.5 Government statistics[2] show that in 1996 there were 3.7 million businesses in the United Kingdom. Of those only 26,000 were medium-sized businesses, *i.e.* had between 50–249 employees and just 7,000 were large, *i.e.* had 250 or more employees.

1.6 Of the 3.7 million businesses, approximately 2.5 million were made up of businesses with no employees. The balance of approximately 1.2 million consists of small businesses employing less than 50 employees in addition to the 33,000 medium-sized and large businesses.

1.7 Small businesses accounted for nearly 46 per cent of non-government employment and 42 per cent of total turnover. The vast majority of these small businesses and indeed a number of medium-sized and large businesses would be classified as family businesses.

1.8 Research carried out by BDO Stoy Hayward in conjunction with London Business School (1990) among the top 8,000

---

[1] Survey carried out by BDO Stoy Hayward in conjunction with Glasgow, Edinburgh and Motherwell Chambers of Commerce 1996/97.
[2] Small and Medium Sized Enterprise Statistics for the United Kingdom 1996.

companies in the United Kingdom indicated that 76 per cent of these businesses are family businesses. Having regard to the overall statistics this must be regarded as a minimum figure. In view of this it is perhaps surprising that it is only recently that family businesses have begun to be recognised as a separate sector with their own particular problems.

In the USA at least 90 per cent[3] of businesses are family owned **1.9** and in Italy the figure is nearer 99 per cent. Research has shown that figures of between 70 and 99 per cent are the norm throughout the developed world. So it is not only in the United Kingdom that family businesses are important.

A recent survey in Central Scotland[4] confirmed figures **1.10** produced in America which show that:

(a) the average life cycle of a family business is 24 years, which coincides with the average tenure of the owner;

(b) only one-third of family businesses reach the second generation;

(c) only 13 per cent survive through to the third generation.

Two facts emerge from all of these statistics: **1.11**

(a) family businesses are extremely important to the economy;

(b) the survival rate of family businesses is poor.

The purpose of this book is to examine the problems which **1.12** are peculiar to family businesses, to look at the effect on the business of family dynamics and to explore ways in which families can be helped to overcome these problems. Hopefully, this will lead to greater survival among family businesses, with the advantageous knock-on effect this will have on the economy.

[3] Ibrahim & Ellis, 1994.
[4] Survey carried out by BDO Stoy Hayward with Glasgow, Edinburgh and Motherwell Chambers of Commerce 1996/97.

CHAPTER 2

FAMILY BUSINESSES—NON-FAMILY BUSINESSES

What is it that differentiates family businesses from other businesses?

In non-family businesses there is one system in operation in **2.1** the management of the business—the business system. Within the family business there are two which are obvious: the family system and the business system. The way the philosophy and culture of owners is influenced by either system has an important effect on the management of the business and on the family. If either system predominates to a large extent, this will cause an imbalance which will either result in relationship problems within the family or have a detrimental effect on the development of the business. Thus, if all decisions are made on the basis of commercial sense, members of the family not involved in that process may well be upset that their interests may not have been taken into account. Conversely, if, for example, a family member who has been unable to find employment has a job created for him in the business, this may not make commercial sense.

Therefore a common-sense approach has to be adopted, **2.2** where a fusing of the two systems can take place. That said, many family businesses take the form of "lifestyle" businesses whose main purpose is to maintain or enhance the lifestyle of the family. In these cases the family position is regarded as of prime importance and, because of this, the businesses tend to progress at a slower pace, being concerned with security and steady growth rather than dramatic growth and risk taking.

5

2.3 Within each family there may well be members of the family
who have different interests in the business. For example,
there are those who work in the business and who obviously
have an interest in retaining the business within the control
of the family as they are dependent on it for their employment
and income. There may well be others in the family who are
not actively involved in the business, but who are dependent
on it for a return on their investment; and there may also be
those within the family who may not wish to retain
ownership of the business, but rather to convert their
ownership into cash. There is therefore a complex interplay
within families which is most easily demonstrated using a
model developed by Davis and Tagiuri (1982) in the USA
(see Figure 2.1).

FIGURE 2.1

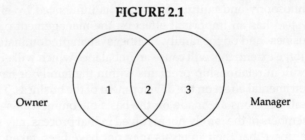

Figure 2.1 represents a non-family business. The two
converging circles represent, on the one hand, management
and, on the other, ownership. As can be seen, there are three
categories of people who share an interest in the business:

(1) owner;
(2) owner manager;
(3) manager.

2.4 Each category has its own differing interests in the business
although in this case, due to the lack of family involvement,
these are fairly clear cut and relatively free of emotional
considerations.

FIGURE 2.2

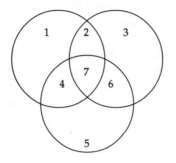

Compare that to Figure 2.2 which shows the effect of adding   **2.5**
an additional circle representing the family. There are now
seven different categories of people, each with different
interests to be satisfied.

In addition to the three mentioned above, the four others   **2.6**
who introduce the family dimension are:

(4) family owner;
(5) family member who is neither an owner nor a
manager;
(6) family member manager;
(7) family member owner manager.

The person who has to deal with all of the problems, both   **2.7**
family and business, is the family member owner manager.
He will normally be the focus where business and family meet.

The problems which he faces are considerable. It is likely that   **2.8**
he will not only be the head of the business but also head of
the family, which places him in the extremely difficult
position of having to reconcile the demands of the family
and of the business.

It is the expectation created in the family which causes major   **2.9**
problems. For example, is it expected that every family

member will be entitled to a job no matter their abilities or, conversely, do parents expect children to enter the business whether or not they want to?

2.10 When considering the position of any member of the family, whether working in the business or not, reference should be made to Figure 2.2 to see where in the model they belong. This will give a much more accurate idea of how they view their interest in the business and therefore the reaction to expect from that person to any proposals being considered for the business.

2.11 Peter Leach[1] states that it is interesting to look at the differences between family systems and business systems. What are the characteristics of the two systems?

Family system	**Business system**
Emotion based	Task based
Subconscious behaviour	Conscious behaviour
Inward looking	Outward looking
Minimising change	Exploiting change

2.12 In a non-family business each of these systems operates independently, but within a family business they operate together and when they overlap tension, friction and problems arise. For example, under the family system a family member employed in the business may well be rewarded not on a system based on performance, but rather on the basis of need. It is also the case that in many family businesses, family members would have what would be regarded as lifetime membership, whereas under the business system, employment within the business would be dependent on performance.

2.13 Under the family system many of the actions are based on subconscious behaviour—for example, fathers wishing to dominate sons and elder sons wanting to dominate younger sons—whereas in the business system people behave in a

---

[1] BDO Stoy Hayward Guide to the Family Business.

much more conscious way based on what is expected of them under their contracts.

The family system encourages introspection by being very **2.14** concerned about looking after family members. Blood is, after all, thicker than water. The business system is more concerned about looking outward to compete in the market place in order to survive in what is a very competitive environment.

Within some family systems change is discouraged, as there **2.15** is no wish to alter structures which have been in place for many years. Within the business system, however, it is important, if the business is to survive, that change is constantly taking place to keep the business efficient and competitive. This is particularly true in the case of new technology where research by Warwick Business School (1997) on behalf of the Stoy Centre for Family Business shows that non-family businesses are more likely to adopt new technology.

If family businesses are to be successful, therefore, they **2.16** require to balance the two systems as far as possible although this can be extremely difficult, if not impossible, to achieve totally.

It is important that areas of potential conflict are identified **2.17** before they occur and systems put in place to deal with them. Transition from one generation to the next is probably the most sensitive time in this respect. This aspect will be dealt with in greater depth in later chapters, but it is important to understand that if succession planning is to be successful it must be started at a very early stage to enable the fullest consultation to take place.

Families tend to operate with a common set of values and **2.18** these, in many cases, are introduced into the business. These values may include:

(a) integrity;
(b) loyalty;
(c) pride in the family name;
(d) ethic of hard work and self sacrifice.

2.19 The introduction of these values brings benefit to the business and helps to strengthen the ties between family and business. So what strengths and weaknesses does being a family business bring to that business?

Strengths

Stability

2.20 Senior management personnel in family businesses tend also to be senior family members, and so they remain in situ for a much longer period than in non-family businesses. Indeed, a recent survey undertaken by BDO Stoy Hayward in conjunction with the London Business School (1990) indicates that 40 per cent of chief executive officers in family businesses have been in office for more than 15 years, while in non-family businesses the figure is 14 per cent. The same survey found that 30.5 per cent of management in family businesses had been in office for over 20 years, whereas in the case of non-family businesses the figure was 6.5 per cent. This contributes towards a much more stable environment.

Long-term planning

2.21 The managers of family businesses tend to take a much longer term view of the business, not having to concern themselves so much about short-term gains. They do not have to be constantly looking at public reaction to their stewardship. This is a very considerable advantage and means that decisions, for example, on capital spend can be made on a long-term return basis rather than on the more pressured basis of looking for a quick return.

Social responsibility and pride

2.22 Family businesses tend to engender loyalty among their employees and customers. They also tend to pay more attention to working conditions, treating long-term employees as an extension to the family. Many family businesses are large employers in their community and place great importance on their position in that community. It is a matter of great pride to them that they are able to support the community in different ways, *e.g.* through participation in local trade associations and local charities and by providing local amenities. This leads, of course, to them wanting to prosper as they do not wish to face their neighbours at the golf club or at the church if they get into difficulties and have, for example, to reduce their workforce to the detriment of the community.

Ability to make decisions quickly

The management of the business is usually tightly held and,   **2.23**
because managers are usually owners, it is much easier to have decisions made more quickly and efficiently.

Commitment

In most cases the family's wealth is tied up in the business,   **2.24**
which is a great incentive for the family to show total commitment to that business. If the business fails, everyone within the family is affected. In addition, and particularly in the case of the founder where the business is very much his own creation, this commitment results in many cases in long hours of hard work and self sacrifice to ensure success.

Weaknesses

Reluctance to change

There is a great temptation in family businesses to say "This is   **2.25**
the way we have always done things and this has been successful in the past, so why change?" This is obviously not conducive to implementing new systems and ideas. It often occurs when the founder is reaching the end of his tenure or when the second or third generation lose momentum because the business is working well. They adopt this attitude, however, at their peril.

As indicated above, the dependence of the family on the business for its wealth and income can lead to a much greater commitment than normal to the business. It can, however, also lead to an aversion to risk-taking in later generations, which can have an extremely detrimental effect on the future growth of the business.

Emotional issues

2.26   Many matters based on the family can be emotionally driven.
When this is applied to the family business it may seem that
decisions are not all made for the best commercial reasons
but are greatly influenced by the family dimension. This can
result in wrong commercial decisions being made to the
detriment of the business.

Succession problems

2.27   As already indicated, one of the most crucial times in the life
of a family business is when ownership of that business is
being transferred from one generation to the next. In a recent
survey carried out in Central Scotland,[2] 47 per cent of owners
indicated that they intended to retire and pass over control
of their business within 10 years. However, only 62 per cent
of those owners had made any retirement provisions and,
indeed, only 50 per cent had even drawn up a will. Most of
those people will have left this matter too late to make any
meaningful planning for retirement possible and may be
forced either to remain dependent on the business for their
income on retirement or to sell the business.

2.28   Having looked at the incumbent's position regarding
financial security after succession, it is interesting to examine
the position of the successor. Those incumbents hoping to
pass over the business in a 6–10-year timespan had only
identified their successors in 44 per cent of the cases and those
anticipating a 0–5-year timespan had identified their
successors in 60 per cent of the cases. These figures highlight
the extent of the problem as planning for succession is a long-
term project which is vital to a successful transition. Planning
is examined in depth in Chapter 4.

Ability to raise capital

2.29   The capital to generate expansion in many family businesses
is generated from within the family. This has a restricting

---

[2]   Survey carried out by BDO Stoy Hayward in conjunction with Glasgow,
Edinburgh and Motherwell Chambers of Commerce 1996/97.

effect on growth—many families have in the past felt happier not borrowing large sums from outside sources, although this attitude is changing.

On the positive side, however, this has helped to give their family businesses a competitive edge over their more highly geared competitors as the cost of borrowing is much less.

Introverted in outlook

Many families are very secretive about their businesses. They **2.30** do not like outsiders, non-family employees and indeed, in some cases, other family members knowing much about them. This lack of communication can lead to many problems arising both inside and outside the family. It can also lead to a reluctance to employ outside professionals, which, as will be seen in a later chapter, can be of considerable disadvantage to the business.

Family businesses, therefore, do differ in many ways from **2.31** non-family businesses as to how they are organised and run. When they are organised properly, having both family and business systems in place, family businesses are very formidable organisations. However, if there is a lack of organisation, communication and proper planning, instead of prospering, family businesses are much more likely to fail. The survey results referred to above, showing that only 33 per cent successfully make the transition from first to second generations and only 13 per cent through to the third, indicate that a lot of work is required if more successful transitions are to be achieved.

CHAPTER 3

MANAGEMENT STAGES

WHAT ARE THE STEPS THROUGH WHICH A FAMILY BUSINESS PASSES
AND DOES EACH STAGE REQUIRE A DIFFERENT APPROACH IN TERMS OF
MANAGEMENT?

Ivan Lansberg of Lansberg, Gersick & Associates illustrates   **3.1**
the transitions from first to second generations and from
second to third generations as shown in Figure 3.1. The
transitions are where, apart from the ownership issues,
problems arise as the style of management required at each
stage has to change to adapt to the differing situations.

FIGURE 3.1

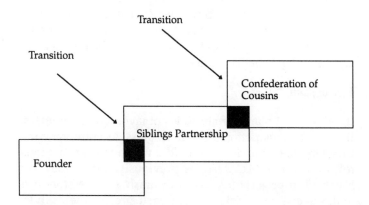

Founder owner manager

Founders of businesses tend to be strong, single-minded,   **3.2**
entrepreneurial people who have the drive and energy to

push the business forward. They are described by Ivan Lansberg as the "John McEnroes" of the business world. Their style of management reflects this, typically following these patterns:

(a) autocratic;
(b) instinctive;
(c) lack of planning.

Autocratic

3.3 Founders, usually being strong, single-minded people who have their own ideas about how to run a business, like to know everything that is going on and tend to be poor delegators. "If you want a job done properly, do it yourself" is how they see things. They supply the drive and do not like to be questioned about their decisions.

Instinctive

3.4 In many cases management training is nil and management decisions are made instinctively "by the seat of the pants". An idea is born in the mind, is developed and put into practice and succeeds, so why go through a formalised rigmarole, is the thought going through his mind. After all, he reasons, he is involved in all aspects of the project and so he knows what is happening. What is the need for complication?

Lack of planning

3.5 It follows that planning ahead is not favoured by founders. It is seen as a restriction on their progress. As entrepreneurs, they tend to be bursting with ideas which they are anxious to put into practice. Also, as previously stated, they are involved in projects from start to finish and therefore can make decisions quickly about each project themselves without involving others.

There is also the point that if forward planning is carried out this will mean that their success rate against what is planned becomes obvious, and founders do not like to publicise their failures.

These management techniques or lack of them, however **3.6** viewed, tend to epitomise the style of founders/entrepreneurs. This style may suit a new business which needs thrust and single-mindedness to progress.

However, when the business reaches a certain size it is not possible for one person to know everything that is going on and so, if the business is to continue to succeed, a change in management style is required.

Sibling partnerships

A change in management style is certainly required when a **3.7** sibling partnership takes over the management of the business. It would be difficult to imagine anything worse than a number of "John McEnroes" trying to run a business together! So the style has to change.

It is important that the management style turns away from **3.8** the autocratic "we'll do things my way" style to one which is more structured along the lines of a partnership. This does not mean that a rigid formal structure is needed at this time but a system of reporting and of communication is required to ensure the smooth operation of the business.

Siblings will have been brought up in the same family **3.9** environment under the same ethical code and so, even if they do not get on with one another, they have a common heritage and know each other's strengths and weaknesses. There is a common bond.

Sibling relationships can be stormy, however, and obviously **3.10** it is in the best interest of the business if, when they take over, careful planning has taken place and each sibling occupies a position in the business in which he is comfortable, thus reducing the potential for possible conflict.

How can this be achieved?

    (a) Open communications—the most important aspect is to ensure that siblings are able to communicate openly with each other. Only in this way can an understanding of each other's point of view be fully understood. If this can be achieved it is likely that siblings will come closer together and be able to work together for the common good.

(b) From those discussions it is equally important that the individual roles are set out for each sibling and that these are agreed by all.

(c) Ownership issues should also be clarified so that there are no problems should the unexpected happen.

(d) There should be a clear policy regarding remuneration, which should be fair to everyone, including non-family employees.

(e) If possible siblings should spend leisure time away from the business together.

(f) Planning should start at the earliest time possible so that full consultation and discussion can take place with the minimum of pressure.

(g) Lastly, it helps if siblings have a sense of humour.

3.11 One of the most difficult tasks is to decide who will be in overall charge of the business and this aspect will be covered in a later chapter. It is mentioned here, because of the importance of this choice.

Confederation of cousins

3.12 When the business moves to the third generation, it is likely that the numbers of family members will increase and so another change in management style is required. Cousins will have been brought up in different families and so there may well be a dilution of family ethics and goals, and indeed these may have been replaced by different ones.

3.13 The additional dilution of ownership and family ethics and goals which comes in most cases with the change necessitates that formal structures are put in place to ensure that they are able to deal with the additional complexities which will arise due to the diverse interests of the cousins. It is probable at this stage that not all cousins will be working in the business and it is important that all interests are considered.

How can this be achieved? Essentially, the interests of the **3.14** business and the family require to be dealt with separately and, to this end, a family council should be set up to deal with the views and needs of the family. This council will comprise of, if the numbers are small enough, all members of the family, or, if not, representatives of the family who will meet on a regular basis to ensure that their interests in relation to the business are looked after.

In most family businesses—certainly during the early stages of **3.15** development—informality is the order of the day. This may even be the case in sibling partnerships. Formal meetings are not held. At this third stage in the business's development, however, informality is no longer acceptable and a formal board of directors should be appointed and properly structured meetings regularly held. Experience shows that family companies which use and appoint non-executive directors to their board are the ones most likely to succeed. The important role of the family outsider will be discussed in greater depth in a later chapter.

Clear rules regarding ownership and employment have to be **3.16** laid down and strictly adhered to and job descriptions and definitions should also be clearly stated. If this is done emotion is, to some extent at least, taken out of the decision-making process.

It is interesting to note that research[1] indicates that businesses **3.17** are far more conscious in providing for the family and obtaining family concessions on key issues as they move down the generations. This may have something to do with the family culture which has developed in the business over the generations and the formalisation of relationships.

Thus, it is clear that the type of management style has to **3.18** change as the business develops through the generations. If it does not do so, the business will most probably fail.

---

[1] BDO Stoy Hayward Survey in conjunction with London Business School, 1990.

CHAPTER 4

THE INCUMBENT

WHAT SHOULD THE INCUMBENT BE CONSIDERING IN THE PERIOD UP
TO TRANSITION?

Succession planning—general

As indicated previously, the most important thing to be done **4.1**
is to plan carefully for succession. Many founders find this a
very difficult period. They have built up a successful business
through their own skills and hard work and, perhaps for the
first time, are now being forced to face their own mortality.
So for incumbents, and indeed for the family as a whole, the
emotional cost is very high.

A recent survey carried out in Central Scotland[1] bears out **4.2**
figures which were produced by a similar survey in the USA
which showed that approximately 50 per cent of incumbents
indicated that they wished the business to be passed on to
the next generation.

So what can be done to make this planning process as simple **4.3**
as possible?

> (a) First, communicate with everyone concerned. This
>   is the single most important step to take and it
>   should be started as early as possible. Surprises
>   cause problems.
> (b) Create a strategic plan for the business encompass-
>   ing the visions of both the incumbent and the

---

[1] Survey carried out by BDO Stoy Hayward in conjunction with Glasgow,
Edinburgh and Motherwell Chambers of Commerce 1996/97.

successor generation. The importance of involving the successor generation in the process cannot be stressed too highly. If they do not share the vision of the future and are not allowed to contribute towards it, it is most unlikely that they will have the heart to implement it and the business will not therefore move forward.

(c) Previous mention was made of a family council to look after the interests of the family, some of whom may not be involved with the management of the family business. It is vital that its views should be recognised when looking at the way forward for the business.

(d) Create a family constitution. This is a document agreed by the family covering such matters as rights of ownership and rights of employment and lays down the rules for the family in connection with the business. It is an extremely important document and will be discussed at length in Chapter 7.

(e) Ensure that key employees who are outwith the family are also involved in the planning process so that they are aware of what is happening. The last thing needed at a time of transition is for key employees to feel that they have been left out in the cold and for them consequently to go seeking alternative employment.

(f) Define very clearly the roles and responsibilities for each of the next generation family employees. Ensure that they have full job descriptions and that provision is made to have their performance monitored in the same way as all employees.

(g) Lastly, but of equal importance, set a firm date for retiral and ensure it is kept to, as target-setting concentrates the mind. All too often good intentions are not always followed up by actions. Many incumbents either delay the "evil day" as they see it or, if they take up a "consultancy" appointment with the business, they believe that their role has not changed. This, of course, places the successor in an extremely difficult position, as it does employees who can be receiving conflicting instructions from each party. This leads to considerable friction and may even result in the downfall of the business.

So much for planning for a normal exit. What happens if the   **4.4**
incumbent or another key family business member dies suddenly? Each family should also have a strategic contingency plan so that, in this event, confusion is kept to a minimum. This plan will deal with such things as:

- (a) Who knows where the important documents are and has access to them?
- (b) Who will take charge of daily operations?
- (c) Who will notify staff, customers and suppliers?
- (d) Who will liaise with the business's advisers?
- (e) What will the immediate effect of the owner's death be upon the banking arrangements?
- (f) Who will see that appointments have to be cancelled or kept?

These are just some of the matters which will arise and will   **4.5**
complicate what is already an extremely fraught time for the family. If plans are made in advance and everyone knows their respective role, this makes life much easier for all concerned.

Dr Bonnie Brown of Transition Dynamics Inc., as part of her   **4.6**
consultation with her clients in the USA, operates a session which she calls "The Family Business Fire Drill". In it she takes all relevant personnel into a room, tells them that the owner has died suddenly, and asks what is to be done and who is going to do it. The reaction can be extremely interesting. It is perhaps something which should be tried in all businesses which are dependent on a very small number of key people.

Will I be financially independent of the business?

In addition to the above matters, the incumbent must look   **4.7**
and see whether he will be financially independent of the business on retirement. If he is to retire from the business it

is important that he has sufficient funds and income outwith the business to ensure that he and his spouse have enough capital and income to live on for the rest of their lives independent of the business. If this is not the case, he will not be in a position to retire and indeed will continue to be dependent on the business for future income. It is likely that in this situation proper transition will not happen as the incumbent will still wish to influence decisions made in the business in order to protect his income.

4.8 An obvious way of providing for retirement is through the setting up of an outside pension fund. One of the problems faced by the founder of the business, however, is that the profits earned tend to be ploughed back into the business thus making it difficult to provide the cash to put into such a fund. This is certainly the case when the business is developing.

4.9 In order for a pension fund to provide the required level of income on retirement it is desirable for contributions to commence at as early a stage as possible. As indicated, however, in view of the requirements of the business, it is often not possible for these payments to be made.

4.10 Other ways therefore have to be found to get around this problem. Too often the easy way out is taken, namely, pay a pension to the retiring incumbent through the business. The consequences of this have already been touched on.

4.11 Another apparently easy way out is for the retiring incumbent to retain his interest in the ownership of the business, relying on the return on capital, that is dividends, to live on. Again, this effectively ensures that transition will not take place until he dies, with all the uncertainty that results from this situation.

4.12 Purchase of own shares by the company is an alternative which may be available. This, of course, is dependent on cash being available within the business and the conditions laid down by law being met. It can, however, provide a capital sum which can either be invested to provide an income or be used to top up a pension policy or to acquire an annuity to help provide income for the retirement years.

It is also possible to set up partial sales of shares to an outside **4.13** funder to provide the necessary capital. An interesting idea, which is becoming more popular, is for the successor generation to buy the business from the incumbent rather than to have it gifted to them and there are fund providers in the market to help in these circumstances.

As previously indicated, a recent survey in Central Scotland[2] **4.14** showed that only 62 per cent of owners whose intention was to retire within 10 years had made any plans for retirement. Time is running out for those who have made no plans and chances are they will probably not be in a position to retire with independent finance when they had hoped.

It is interesting to note that 57 per cent of those who had **4.15** made no plans said they were too busy, 18 per cent said that it was due to lack of information, 21 per cent said that they were not aware of the importance, and 4 per cent said that cost was the influencing factor. Looking behind those figures a cynic could say that many respondents have no intention of considering retirement, believing, one assumes, in their own immortality.

Who will succeed in management?

One of the most difficult tasks is to decide who will take over **4.16** the mantle of running the business. Who is to be in charge? The opportunity for family conflict in this area is considerable and in many cases the incumbent shies away from discussing the matter in order to maintain peace in the family. Indeed, in a recent Scottish survey[3] successors had only been identified in 44 per cent of the cases where the incumbents wished to retire within 10 years. This denies the successor their promotion while at the same time stoking up family

---

[2] Survey carried out by BDO Stoy Hayward in conjunction with Glasgow, Edinburgh and Motherwell Chambers of Commerce 1996/97.
[3] *ibid.*

tensions in the interim period due to the uncertainty which is created.

4.17 Historically the eldest son was the automatic choice to lead the next generation whether or not he was the most capable. This, of course, led to a dreadful waste of talent should one of the younger sons or daughters be more able. Attitudes are, however, changing. More and more businesses are selecting the most able successor to take over the mantle from the older generation whether from family or not. Great care has to be taken, however, if this is to happen without friction and rancour. This is a difficult process usually requiring help.

4.18 In a recent situation, where a son and a daughter were employed in the family business, the incumbent decided that the daughter should take over as managing director. Unfortunately, no consultation took place and the decision was announced to the world without either of the siblings being previously aware of it. It transpired that the son had had aspirations for the position and he was obviously extremely upset and angry—so much so that he refused to co-operate with the new managing director and the business eventually had to be sold.

4.19 As previously stated, communication is the key. This is not a decision to be made only by the incumbent. The next leaders have to have the approval and support of their generation and so they must have an input into the decision. If discussions had taken place in the above case over a reasonable period and with all parties concerned having been given their say, the reasons for the appointment could have been explained and any counter-argument considered. Instead, a dictatorial decision was made with the resultant unfortunate consequences.

Who will succeed in ownership?

4.20 It is important that at this stage ownership is separated from management. Not all of the next generation may be active in the business. In the case of limited companies this is relatively simple to achieve as ownership can be readily changed by transferring shares. In partnerships and sole traders, however, ownership and management are very much tied together as the risk element ensures that all owners are very involved in management decisions being made. At this point in the business's development, therefore, consideration should be given to converting to a limited company if this has not already been done. Whatever the pros and cons from a business perspective, the limited company separates out, on paper, ownership from management.

There is a very strong feeling among families that it is important to be "fair" to the next generation. Being "fair" in many cases equates to every sibling receiving the same proportion of shares or ownership of the business in their parents' estates. **4.21**

Is this, however, actually being "fair"? If some of the siblings are working in the business and some are not, is it "fair" that each should receive the same proportion of shares? Only if the family understand the issues it will raise. **4.22**

Those working in the business may no doubt take the view that profits should be retained in the business to help finance future growth while those outwith the business, not unreasonably, may take the view that profits should be, to a large extent, distributed by way of dividend. It is easy to see how difficulties can arise between active and non-active members of the family in this scenario. **4.23**

It is also easy to see that if non-active members of the family control the majority of ownership, which can also be a result of this policy, this can cause considerable problems for the active owners. **4.24**

Great care has therefore to be taken in deciding the future ownership of the business. There is no general right or wrong solution. Each family has to establish its own rules, with which it is comfortable. **4.25**

The importance of discussion among family members has already been stressed. This is another area where all parties **4.26** involved should be able to have an input into the discussions and be part of the decision-making process so that there are no surprises. Consideration should also be given to ensure that the effect of any decisions made on future generations is taken into account. If a wrong decision is made now, the effect on relationships in future generations can be catastrophic. Most families require help to discuss these issues and to reach an agreement.

4.27 Many families do take the view that ownership of the business can only go to those who are active in the business. Indeed, in many cases ownership is further restricted to those in the blood line, spouses and in-laws being excluded.

4.28 If this situation is to prevail, careful judgement has to be given to the mechanics of this, as well as to how non-active members are to have their inheritances equalised. For example, what happens to his shares when an active member leaves the business, or how does a new active member acquire shares on joining? These are practical problems which should be dealt with in the family constitution.

4.29 An ideal solution for some families could be that only active members of the family should own the business while the inheritance of the non-active family members is equalised by using assets which are not part of the business, *e.g.* house, stock exchange investments, etc. Obviously, however, this will not be possible in all cases, *e.g.* where the business represents the main wealth of the family.

4.30 Equally, a family may be more comfortable if ownership passes to all next generation members whether active in the business or non-active. Rules on how potential conflicts between active and non-active members are to be handled will have to be carefully thought out and laid down, preferably in advance in a family constitution.

4.31 It is possible to carry out a reorganisation of the structure of the business, *e.g.* the capital could be split between voting and non-voting shares with the voting shares held by those active in the business. The non-voting shares could be coupon shares giving a stated dividend each year, which may satisfy the non-active members.

Another device which could be used to equalise inheritance **4.32** between active and non-active family members, if the active members are to inherit the business, is by way of life insurance with policies equal to the value of the business, written on behalf of the non-active members by the incumbents. This, however, will very much depend on the health of the incumbent and their foresight to set this up years in advance.

Trusts can also be set up to hold interests in businesses if, for **4.33** example, the incumbent still wishes to retain some control over the business while at the same time wanting to avoid direct ownership himself. It is possible for the grantor to be one of the trustees in a trust set up by himself. There are obviously legal and taxation implications if this route is chosen and, therefore, detailed specialist advice is required in looking at each situation.

As previously mentioned, those taking over the management **4.34** and ownership of the business may acquire the ownership at value in what is becoming known as a family buy-out. Any moneys received by the incumbents are then available for them to live on and will form part of their estates for all family members. This is an area which is becoming more popular.

There are therefore many varied ways for ownership of the **4.35** business to be transferred. This should only be done after very careful planning has taken place including extensive communication among family members. If possible, the rules regarding ownership should be agreed and set out in the family constitution, which will be dealt with in depth in a later chapter.

CHAPTER 5

THE PROSPECTIVE SUCCESSOR

Matters to be considered by a prospective successor

Like the choice of a spouse, whether or not to join the business **5.1**
is one of the most important decisions a prospective successor
will make in his lifetime. It is vital, therefore, that many
considerations are taken into account by him and that the
decision is only made after a reasonable period of reflection
and with no outside pressures. In a recent Central Scotland
survey,[1] where the incumbent hopes to retire within 6–10
years, 57 per cent of possible successors indicated that they
wished to be involved in the business, the balance having
decided not to join or being undecided. This figure is perhaps
surprising to a number of people who may have anticipated
that a larger proportion would have wished to join the family
business. However, more and more children are moving on
to higher education and have not decided at this stage
whether or not they do wish to join the business.

The reasons for wanting to join are important. Is he going to **5.2**
join because of parental pressure? In many cases parents
expect the children to join the business, in other words what
is known as "golden handcuffs" will apply. The matter is not
discussed but the expectation is there and, therefore, the
prospective successor joins the business not because he wants
to but because he does not want to disappoint his parents. If
this is the case and his heart is not in it, such a move is
probably doomed from the start.

---

[1] Survey carried out by BDO Stoy Hayward in conjunction with Glasgow,
Edinburgh and Motherwell Chambers of Commerce 1996/97.

5.3 Is his joining the business seen by the prospective successor as the easy option? Does he anticipate stepping into the business at a fairly senior level without having to bother about much training or effort and be the "boss"? In order to ensure that this does not happen, it is important that certain ground rules are laid down regarding employment within the business. These will be covered as each point is dealt with in turn.

5.4 The first important things to be considered are does he have an interest in the business and what does he believe he can bring of value to it? If the answer to these fundamental questions is positive, then he should move on to consider more detailed questions.

5.5 Is there a worthwhile job available in the business which he could fill competently, or is a job being created for him? It often happens in family businesses that jobs are created for the next generation. This is not a recommended way forward for a number of reasons. The job will in all probability be without proper definition and also without the prospects for advancement. There is also a strong possibility that it will engender resentment among non-family employees who will see it exactly as it is, namely an artificial position which may in some way affect the overall efficiency of the business and also the promotion ladder. It is therefore extremely important that any job on offer is a proper position which is required by the business and when rules are being laid down for the family constitution it should be made very clear within that document that no jobs will be created purely for family reasons.

5.6 Will there be a proper training regime in place? Training is a very important part in any job and it is perhaps even more important for family members who have aspirations to leadership within the business to have proper training programmes in place for them. When incumbents hoping to retire within 6–10 years were asked in a recent survey in Central Scotland[2] if their prospective successors had the skills required, only 64 per cent believed that

---

[2] Survey carried out by BDO Stoy Hayward in conjunction with Glasgow, Edinburgh and Motherwell Chambers of Commerce 1996/97.

they did have these skills. There is, therefore, a considerable amount of work to be done in this field.

There is a train of thought which says that it is important for family members joining the business to "start at the bottom", meaning that they should start as office boys or sweeping up in the factory. In this way, so the theory goes, they learn all the jobs in the business which is good education for their future. But is it? Successful businesses, and certainly those from second generation onwards, are usually run by teams of specialists in their own fields. Is it not better, therefore, that they should be trained in the area in which they will operate, *e.g.* technical, finance or selling, backed up by general managerial competence? In this way much more benefit will flow to the business where management members can develop their own particular skills. **5.7**

He must consider whether he would enjoy the challenge of a job outwith the family business in preference to joining that business. Some family members may feel that joining the family firm is the easy option and that they would rather prove themselves in the outside world. **5.8**

Even if he decides to join the family firm it is recommended that the successor obtains outside experience if possible. The Central Scotland survey showed that in cases where the incumbent wished to retire in 6–10 years, only 43 per cent of potential successors had any outside experience at all. This percentage is worryingly low. Outside experience is important for several reasons.

(a) He makes his mistakes at someone else's expense and so avoids family recriminations.

(b) He gains experience outwith the family in another environment.

(c) He sees how other businesses work and so will be able to bring new ideas to the family business.

(d) He gains experience in what it is like to be an employee which will help him to widen his knowledge and understanding of how his employees will feel and react when he joins management in the family business.

(e) His experience may confirm to him that working for his father may not be as bad as he thought!

When drawing up the family constitution thought should be given to having a requirement for family members to work outwith the family business prior to joining.

5.9 The relationships within the family will play an important part in the decision-making process.

    (a) Are these relationships good?
    (b) Will the successor be able to work with his father?
    (c) Will he be able to work with his siblings?
    (d) It is certain that differences of opinion will occur. Are methodologies in place to resolve these differences?

5.10 Gaining the respect of the non-family members is important if he is eventually to command a senior management post. It is vital that any promotion is gained through merit and not through family patronage. It is equally important that he enjoys the same conditions as any other employee of equal rank. This is particularly true in terms of salary and benefits. In addition, his work should be appraised on the same basis as all employees. There is nothing worse for losing respect and damaging morale within the business, than if a family member enjoys much better working conditions than his non-family peers. The prospective successor must consider this prior to making his decision.

5.11 It is desirable, if possible, for the family member to have a mentor who is not a member of the family, *e.g.* non-executive director or manager who he can turn to for advice when required. In this way the difficulty of discussing problems with, say, his father can be eliminated. Father/son rivalry is well known and it can be very difficult for some matters to be discussed rationally between them. The same situation pertains to sibling rivalry. So if problems can be dealt with and advice sought outwith the family circle, so much the better. Any possible successor should therefore look at the business and see if there is anyone within its ranks who could fill that role.

The future ownership of the business will also be an important **5.12**
issue to consider.

   (a) Will ownership rest with those who work in the
       business?
   (b) If so, what arrangements have been made for those
       who join and exit from the business?
   (c) What is the position of those family members
       outwith the business in terms of equalising their
       share of their parents' estates?

All of these ownership issues can create dreadful family **5.13**
problems if not handled correctly and any prospective
successor should wish to know what is in the mind of the
incumbent in relation to these matters prior to making any
decision about joining the business. The last thing he wants
to be faced with is a family battle over ownership when he
has settled into managing the business.

As can be seen, therefore, the decision on whether or not to **5.14**
join the family business is not one to be taken lightly and it
certainly should not been seen as an easy option. If the
business is to prosper it is important that the correct people
are put in place within the organisation and if these are to be
family members they should first want to join the business
and secondly be able to contribute to its future success
through their ability.

CHAPTER 6

OUTSIDERS

In Chapter 2 attention was drawn to the fact that family **6.1** businesses tend to be introverted. There can be an unwillingness to change coupled with an unhappiness at any outside involvement in the business. There may be a feeling that only those family members actively involved in management need to know anything about the business.

Research, however, shows that the family businesses which **6.2** employ outsiders and are open to the advice and ideas that outsiders bring to the business, are more likely to survive and succeed. The role of the outsider is therefore one of importance to the business. It is interesting to note, however, that in a recent survey carried out by Warwick Business School on behalf of the Stoy Centre for Family Business (1997) only 9 per cent of family unquoted companies had non-executive directors compared to 19 per cent of non-family unquoted companies.

Outside involvement takes several forms: **6.3**

    (a) non-family managers;
    (b) non-executive directors;
    (c) advisers.

Non-family full-time managers

In Chapter 3 consideration was given to the different styles **6.4** of management as a family business develops in relation to family members. As it grows, however, it is unlikely that competent family members will be available to fill all of the management roles required. This situation obviously depends on how quickly the business grows, but can arise at any time in relation to any position within the business— even chief executive officer. He is, after all, just as liable to sudden death as the rest of the population!

6.5 Thought must be given, therefore, to the introduction of non-family employees in the form of professional managers to fill these roles. This process is known as "professionalising the business" and it is vital that the necessity for this is recognised when the need arises.

6.6 This can be an extremely difficult process for a family business to adopt. It is particularly difficult when the business grows rapidly under the founder, when steps have to be taken to expand the management structure and no competent family members are available. As previously stated, one of the matters which founders find difficult is delegation. In addition there may be a fear that, by bringing non-family management into the business, this will result in a loss of control by the family.

6.7 It is important at this stage to stress that if both family and outsiders are to be comfortable with their roles, the business should be structured correctly, separating management and ownership. If this does not happen the outsider may feel that he is being dragged into family politics and the family may feel that the outsider is being involved in matters which are not his concern. In either case, this could well lead to friction.

6.8 In terms of recruitment it can be difficult for family businesses to attract suitable managers from outwith the family. There is always the suspicion that family members will be favoured in respect of working terms and conditions and also promotion, and this tends to put off prospective candidates. The importance of having a level playing field in relation to these matters between family members and non-family members cannot be stressed too much if a manager of suitable calibre is to be attracted.

6.9 A non-family manager can obviously bring with him experience and a knowledge of other businesses and a perspective which is not influenced by being a family member. If this experience and knowledge are to be properly utilised, however, he must be involved in detailed planning and have available all the necessary information within the business. As can be seen, therefore, the influence of non-family managers tends to open up the management of the business and make it more outward looking.

As business structures become more developed and the business grows, the role of the non-family manager may well become more important. Ownership among the family may have spread to encompass family members who are not employed in the business and this should result in a much more formal approach to management giving more prominence to the non-family manager. **6.10**

Non-executive directors

As previously stated it is much easier to separate ownership and management in a limited company than a sole trade or partnership. This is because of the liability situation where management decisions in a sole trade or a partnership directly affect the liability of that sole trader or partner. Reference has already been made to the fact that when a business reaches a certain stage in its development, if it has not already become a limited company, then consideration should be given to this issue. However, it is important to stress this again. **6.11**

The disciplines which should be enforced by being a limited company should ensure a more formal approach to management. A board of directors should be appointed and formal board meetings should be held. It has to be said, however, that in many family companies this does not always happen. The board is a nominal body and meetings tend to be less than formal with no regular times set, no agenda and no minutes kept. **6.12**

As the business develops, the need for formality increases. A properly qualified board is required which meets on a regular basis with proper agendas, reporting requirements for the individual members and proper minutes being taken. **6.13**

6.14 Something which adds greatly to the authority of the board is the appointment of a non-executive director. He would ideally be a business man of proven ability who can bring a whole new dimension to the board. In many cases, he will be a person who has been successful in running his own business or has reached a senior position in a larger business and has retired early on favourable pension terms. Thus, finance is not his driving force. He is mainly interested in job satisfaction.

6.15 He is able to contribute the following to the board:

    (a) outside experience giving other points of view for consideration in the decision-making process;

    (b) a different range of contacts from those known to the family;

    (c) act as an independent adviser to any member of the family. It can be particularly useful for him to act as a mentor to family members who have started in the business and are finding their way. As previously indicated, it is often easier for them to discuss their problems and seek advice from a non-family member;

    (d) an expertise which may not be available within the present executive management;

    (e) an independent view which is not influenced by reliance on a full-time salary. Being free of financial reliance is a very important factor in considering objectivity.

6.16 Non-executive directors have the same legal responsibilities as executive directors and so have to be extremely careful about the business they are joining. Obviously the viability of the business is extremely important, but the prospective non-executive director will also be very interested in the organisation present within the business. He will want to see that responsibilities are clearly defined and that proper structures for reporting and communication are in place. If this is not so, the chances are he will decline the appointment.

6.17 The appointment of a suitable non-executive director to the board adds gravitas to it. It indicates to the family and to the outside world that the executive are serious in their intention to take the business forward. However, as evidenced by the survey indicated previously, very few family businesses have taken advantage of the services of a non-executive director— a position which will hopefully improve.

Advisers

If advisers are chosen carefully they too can bring an extra **6.18** dimension to the business. Many of them have very considerable experience covering a large number of businesses, which can be made available to family businesses.

However, care has to be taken to ensure that the advisers **6.19** have experience in the areas where their advice is required. This is not always the case and it is important, first, for the adviser to admit his limitations and, secondly, for the client not to feel that he will make do through a feeling of loyalty, however honourable that may be.

One other major aspect which affects the advice given to **6.20** family businesses by advisers is that the technically correct advice is not only the proper advice in the circumstances. It is important that the adviser is fully aware of all the ramifications before advice is offered. He must be fully aware of the position within the family and this must be taken into account in any advice given. Many advisers are reluctant to become involved in family matters which they see as none of their business. However, the resolution of many problems within family businesses cannot be successfully carried through on technical advice alone and in order to get to the root of many of these problems an understanding of the family position is vital.

Communication among advisers is also extremely important. **6.21** Experience shows that if they can work together as teams this is in the best interest of the family business. This can be illustrated as follows.

The family solicitor may be asked to draw up a will by the **6.22** founder. This solicitor has not been involved in the preparation of the articles of association or a family constitution and so is unaware of their terms. He advises his client that it is in his best interest to leave his estate, including the shares in the family business, to his widow and the will is drawn up accordingly. However, in the family constitution or the articles of association there is a clause which indicates that shares in the family company can only be inherited by members of the blood line. A conflict therefore arises which will probably require further legal action to resolve, if it remains as at the present when the founder dies. This problem could have been resolved had there been proper communication between the advisers. If they had worked as a team and consideration had been given to all those relevant matters at the one time, the problem would not have arisen.

6.23 Outsiders play a large part in the onward development of family businesses if the right people are chosen, but the choice is vital and the businesses themselves must be ready to accept the experience and advice which outsiders bring to them.

CHAPTER 7

THE FAMILY CONSTITUTION

The previous chapter gave an example of a trap that might **7.1** capture a business family and their unwary advisers. Many couples opt for "sweetheart wills" in which each leaves their estate to the other. In the example given, this arrangement came up against the obstacle of a business constitution which prohibited transfer of ownership to spouses or partners.

Advisers who combine an understanding of family systems **7.2** with the necessary array of technical skills are best equipped to help business families avoid these problems. The technical competencies of family business solicitors should include estate planning, company and partnership law, property, employment law, matrimonial and family law, pensions and tax. This knowledge then needs to be applied creatively to ensure the needs of the business and the family are identified, balanced and, of course, written down.

Every family business will have some legal documents, **7.3** somewhere. Oblivion is their usual fate until, inevitably, something happens whereupon the documents are consulted and—almost as inevitably—are found to be wanting.

This state of affairs is undesirable and avoidable. It is essential **7.4** for the health of the family and the business that legal affairs are kept in order to reflect the changing needs and circumstances as well as to take account of legislation changes. At the very least the articles of association of the family company or the family partnership agreement should be reviewed regularly. Sole traders will not have any constitutional document of this type but like the members of a family company or partnership they require legal and taxation planning advice on their estate as well as assistance in the technical areas referred to above.

7.5 There is an additional document which is unique to family businesses and which many families find helpful. This is the family constitution.

What is a "Family Constitution"?

7.6 The family constitution sets out the principles and practices to be followed by successive generations of a business family with regard to ownership and management of the business. The content of the constitution should address the issues that are highlighted by the model introduced in paragraph 2.5 and shown again at Figure 7.1.

FIGURE 7.1

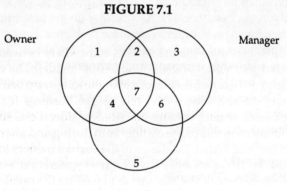

Owner   Manager

1 2 3

7

4 6

5

Family

7.7 Apart from being a useful guide in creating a family constitution, this model should highlight the futility of an approach that pretends that business decisions will always be made only for business reasons and will not be influenced by the overlapping family system.

OWNERSHIP OF THE BUSINESS

"Custodian" or "value-out"

7.8 The owners of a family business are often patient about receiving a return on their investment. This "patient capital" can give the business a significant financial and strategic advantage over other businesses where the demand for return means capital is more expensive to raise and short-term achievements take precedence over long-term strategic goals.

In some cases families view ownership as being held "in trust" for succeeding generations. It is accepted that the primary responsibility of ownership is to ensure that the business is passed on rather than conferring a right to receive income or the opportunity to realise capital by selling the business.   **7.9**

In contrast to this type of "custodian ownership" other families want, even expect, value to be extracted from the business. The "value-out" model sees the business primarily as a means of providing for the current owners with little concern being given to passing the business on to the next generation.   **7.10**

For many families the ideal exists somewhere between the "custodian" model and the "value-out" model. The desire to create a sustainable enterprise for the long-term benefit of the family, and others who rely on the business for their livelihoods, is tempered by practical considerations such as the financial needs of the owners both during and after their working lives. Also, the desire of the current owners to pass on the business assumes that the next generation want to become owners. If there is a wish to pass on the ownership, it raises the question of the type of owners the family wants in the business.   **7.11**

"Active" or "passive" owners?

Those in segment 7 in the model are usually described as "active" owners; in other words, they work in the business. In contrast, those in segment 4 who do not work in the business can be described as "passive" owners.   **7.12**

As mentioned in Chapter 4, it is easy to imagine the different views on ownership that are likely to be held by active owners and passive owners. The former will be more concerned   **7.13** about reinvesting profits while passive owners will have a keen interest in the same profits being distributed by way of a dividend. The family constitution can set out the family's agreed policy in this area thereby helping to avoid damaging conflicts.

7.14 It is worth mentioning that passive ownership is very unlikely in a family partnership. Since partners have unlimited personal liability for the debts of the firm, it is unwise for any partner to be detached from the day-to-day management of the partnership.

Transfer of ownership

7.15 The family's views on the nature of ownership "custodian" or "value-out", "active" or "passive", will directly affect the rules governing transfer of ownership. Selling out may be prohibited because the family has determined that ownership is a long-term commitment and responsibility. If sale is permitted, it may be specified that it can only be to other active family members or to any family members whether or not they work in the business. It must be remembered that the more restricted the class of potential purchasers, the more difficult it may be to find anyone able or willing to acquire an ownership share that another family member wants, or needs, to sell.

7.16 The above assumes that, whatever happens, it is only family members who can acquire an ownership interest in the business. This raises two further matters for the family to consider.

7.17 First, what does "family" mean? In this context is the term used to identify the extended family, including spouses and partners, or is it restricted to bloodline descendants of the founder? If transfer to spouses/partners is permitted, a policy should be in place to say what happens if relationships break down.

7.18 Secondly, if the needs of the business dictate that an "outsider" has to be recruited, as indicated in Chapter 6, an ownership stake might be needed to attract the best candidate. The same issues arise where the business needs an injection of outside capital—for example, from a venture capitalist.

Every member of a family business will have strong views **7.19** on these matters which will inevitably come into the open at some stage. It is undoubtedly preferable for there to be a policy in place before the issue arises and for the family's agreement on the matter to be set out clearly in the family constitution.

MANAGEMENT OF THE BUSINESS

Management in every business faces many challenges. In **7.20** addition it was explained in Chapter 3 that as the ownership of a family business changes, its management needs to cope with some unique issues.

Therefore, it is interesting that the way in which a family **7.21** business is managed is frequently the result of evolution rather than design. Sometimes this works but equally it can lead to haphazard decision-making and the repetition of inherited patterns of behaviour that no longer best serve the business or the family.

"Professionalising" the business

In Chapter 6 we dealt with the term "professionalising the **7.22** business" which is often used to describe the changes that occur, or at least should occur, as the family business develops. The constitution can record the family's acknowledgment of this need and set out a clear system of governance—for example, regular management meetings— that is responsive to business needs and respects the important role of the family.

However, it is a mistake to adopt a rigid "business first" or **7.23** "family first" approach as each is likely to fail both the business and the family on certain occasions. Take, for example, the issue of employing family.

7.24   It is common to find that the different roles involved in owning and managing the family business become blurred. This can be particularly sensitive when those who have inherited ownership find it difficult to accept that they have not inherited or otherwise acquired the skills needed to run the business.

Employing family

7.25   To the current and the next generations, entry to the business may be a source of hope, a threat or an agonising frustration. The decision whether or not to employ a family member can leave expectations unfulfilled and relationships in tatters. A clear policy that is consistently applied can be of immense benefit to the business and the family.

The policy could set out the following:

- **Who is eligible to join the business?**

  For example some families prefer not to employ spouses and in-laws.

- **What entry criteria apply?**

  The vast majority of business families adhere to the view that the business is not to be seen as an informal job creation scheme for the family. Family members should be employed only if there is a business need and they possess the necessary skills and experience. The policy in the constitution can set out guidelines on age, education and experience that family members need before applying to join the business. However, the policy may contain a direction that it be applied compassionately, especially where a family member has special needs.

- **Job application procedure**

  It is preferable where possible that direct family do not take part in the selection process. This principle can be usefully extended to supervision in the business so that the contribution made by a family member can be objectively monitored.

• **Remuneration package**

  Especially where family members employed in the business are also owners, it is valuable to make clear the rewards and benefits that flow from employment as distinct from the return on investment. This helps the business to adopt a proper remuneration policy and to avoid dissatisfaction among non-family employees who are important to the business.

As already mentioned a successful management strategy for a family business needs to be clear on the separate roles of management and family.   **7.26**

THE FAMILY

Traditionally many advisers to family businesses have made the impossible demand of their clients that family issues should be kept out of the business. It is difficult to see how the best advice and assistance can be given to the family business by ignoring the business family.   **7.27**

Communication is the lubricant that helps every family and every business to operate efficiently. While every family and every business will have communication bottlenecks, these being another task for management to resolve, careful planning can help to avoid such blockages occurring between the business and the family.   **7.28**

The aim must surely be to reach a state where the family knows what to expect of the business and the business knows what to expect of the family. The family constitution is ideal for setting out how this state can be achieved.   **7.29**

Going back to the model, everyone in segments 4, 5, 6 and 7 has an interest that should be represented. Those in segment 5, family not directly involved in the business, should not be excluded; they have "sweat equity" in the business which is   **7.30** often hard earned as they take the brunt of the frustrations and concerns of those working in the day-to-day business. Therefore every family member is likely to have an opinion on some or all of the following matters:

(a) sustaining family ownership;
(b) succession in leadership;
(c) the professional management of the business, including employing family, as referred to above;
(d) wealth creation for the family and sustainable growth for the business;
(e) cultivating family values including family harmony and a commitment to the business.

7.31 Reaching a consensus on these and many other matters besides needs time and a way of allowing everyone a voice in the discussions. To this end the family could hold its own sessions which are most likely to be successful if structured and conducted as proper meetings.

7.32 It is unlikely that this will be a one-off event. Therefore, the family might wish to have regular get-togethers to review policy in these areas. The management of the business, especially where this includes outsiders, will probably draw strength from the fact that the family is dealing with these matters in a coherent and constructive manner. Both the family and the management might feel it would be worthwhile to take matters further and, as suggested in Chapter 3, have a family council made up of family members which co-ordinates these affairs and, where appropriate, represents the family's views on certain issues to management.

How to create a family constitution

7.33 The creation of a document of such importance to a family business takes time and commitment from everyone involved. It is vital that all the issues are resolved and this may take a considerable time, even a number of years, to achieve. It must also be realised that the process may not always be a comfortable experience.

The family must be willing to stick with a process designed **7.34**
to provide a structured opportunity for everyone to assess,
organise and clarify the relationship between the family and
the business. The services of advisers skilled in facilitating
this type of process will be a valuable investment in the future
for the business and the family.

Creating the constitution should be grasped as a new **7.35**
beginning and not as an end in itself. The document should
be reviewed regularly and contain a clear procedure for
making amendments. While privacy and confidentiality are
necessary to ensure the process can be open and transparent,
the family could decide that the existence of the constitution
does not need to be kept a secret. Indeed it might be decided
that those with a stake in the business—employees,
customers, suppliers and the advisers/bank—would draw
strength and confidence from the existence of the constitution.

A family constitution will help the business and the family **7.36**
to fulfil their strategic potential. If the process of creating the
constitution is carefully and professionally managed, it will
assist the family and the business to navigate to where they
want to be in the future. The constitution will improve the
prospects of a successful transition to the next generation by
preserving what is best in the family and the business.

CHAPTER 8

BANKING AND THE FAMILY BUSINESS

Family businesses often see their banks as something to be **8.1**
avoided and to be kept in the dark about their business as
much as possible. This is an attitude which has developed
over the years but is most unhelpful in terms of building a
relationship with their banker and developing trust, which
is a vital part of this relationship.

It is important for business families to understand the criteria **8.2**
under which banks operate.

Banks are increasingly stressing the importance of the **8.3**
relationship between their managers and their business
customers. For this approach to be effective, there must be
open communication between a bank and its business
customers. The concept of a bank working in partnership
with the business has grown in acceptance. Businesses should
not be wary of this approach.

How can this relationship be developed? **8.4**

    (a) In selecting a bank ensure that the manager dealing
with the business has experience in its sector and
knows the business. In this way he will be able to
give useful advice and add value to the traditional
banking relationship.

    (b) Banking is a relationship of trust which is a two-
way process. If businesses expect assistance and
advice from their bankers, they must be prepared
to spend time keeping the bank informed of
developments within the business.

    (c) As far as possible always keep agreements which have been made. If a problem arises and it is likely that an agreement will be broken, inform the bank immediately and try to renegotiate the terms.

    (d) If bad news is being presented to the bank, also present the solution or action which is being taken to remedy the position.

    (e) Keep the bank informed of the plans for the business and the likely impact on cash balances.

8.5 Businesses are nowadays being asked to produce more and more information to their banks. The information required will be defined largely by the level of risk which the bank perceives in the business. The greater the perceived risk or the higher the potential loss to the bank, the greater amount of information the bank will seek from the business. The basic minimum which the bank will require will be a copy of the annual accounts, but as it increases its need to monitor the activity of a business, it will ask for copies of management accounts and possibly details of customer and supplier balances. The frequency with which this information is to be provided will increase to half-yearly, quarterly or even monthly, again depending on the perceived risk.

Proper financing of your business

8.6 Most businesses have a characteristic cash flow profile and it is important that this is identified. An extreme example would be a fireworks manufacturer. Such a business would probably have very low sales for most of the year with very high sales in August and September as shops stock up before November 5. The cash flow profile is likely to start as very cash rich in early December as the receipts from the sales leading up to November 5 are collected. The cash balance will then decline steadily as the company meets the costs of producing a new stock of fireworks. It is likely that the business would have a large overdraft by October of the following year, just before it is able to collect its cash receipts from sales. This is illustrated in Figure 8.1.

FIGURE 8.1

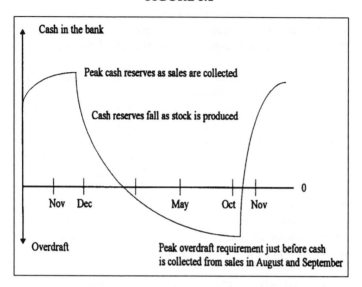

The funding requirements of the business should be matched **8.7** to the cash profile. Therefore, in the example above, the fireworks manufacturer will require to fund a peak borrowing requirement at October each year.

If the business has a cash requirement because it has made **8.8** losses, it will be harder to explain to the bank why the overdraft facility should be increased. In this case it is important to demonstrate to the bank that this has been recognised and that appropriate actions have been identified to resolve the problems. The banking relationship is primarily one of trust and, secondly, one of confidence. If the bank loses confidence in the ability of management either to manage the business or to react properly to commercial problems, it will be very difficult to rebuild the goodwill once enjoyed. Therefore, as soon as it becomes apparent that there will be a breach of an overdraft limit or a failure to make payments on a term loan, the bank should be advised immediately. In meeting with the bank to discuss any trading problems, it is important always to be honest about the situation and present viable and sensible solutions.

8.9   Different methods of finance should be used in relation to different assets such as: (1) permanent fixed assets, land or buildings; (2) other fixed assets, plant or machinery and vehicles; (3) current assets such as stock and debtors.

8.10   In general the overdraft facility should only be used to fund working capital, as it is repayable on demand. Therefore, if a business is using its overdraft facilities to fund asset purchases, it is using up its available working capital. A general rule of thumb is that the overdraft should be no more than 10 per cent of turnover. If a business's overdraft account is not regularly in credit in line with the cash cycle of the business, then consideration should be given to restructuring the borrowing. As an alternative to overdraft, the financing of the debtor's portion of working capital may be carried out by factoring and invoice discounting, and the bank manager will be able to advise on this.

8.11   Financing fixed assets or any hard-core element of working capital is normally best achieved by a term loan. This form of financing will try to spread the loan payments over the estimated cash generative life of the asset. The form and timing of the repayments can now be structured to suit the individual asset or business.

8.12   Plant, machinery and vehicles are frequently financed by leasing or hire-purchase as the leasing and hire-purchase companies are often able to offer better rates of interest than conventional bank finance.

Assessment of risk

8.13   A bank will assess the overall risk attached to any proposal by examining the component parts of a business and the external factors influencing the performance of that business in its chosen market. Banks will review a business in the light of different types of risk and obviously a bank will try to minimise the overall risk. If the perceived risk in any one area of assessment is high, then the other types of risk will normally require to be minimal. Banks will also look for security to further minimise or eliminate risk as far as possible. In general terms, the higher the perceived risk, the higher the margin or interest rate that the bank will want to charge.

Asset risk

This is an assessment of the amount of money which a bank **8.14** is willing to lend on the security of the assets of the business. Assessment is based on the amount which is conservatively estimated would be recovered by the sale of those assets. Any deterioration in the assets or in the prevailing market value of those assets increases the risk to the bank. This is why banks will frequently ask for revaluations of property and require details of the insurances for any assets.

Trading risk

This is an assessment of the future cash flows of the business. **8.15** It is essential that, over a given period of time, every business should be cash generative. It is possible for a profitable company to fail simply because it runs out of cash. Therefore, it is unable to pay its debts as they fall due and it is technically insolvent. A bank would hope to have a minimal trading risk. The more uncertain or speculative the cash flow, then the greater the risk that the bank will perceive. Therefore, most high technology or research companies are funded by investors' funds and not by bank debt.

Commercial or industry risk

This is an assessment of the market sector in which the **8.16** business operates. The bank will form a view on the products, market share, competitors and customers of the business. All of these will have an impact on the level of risk which the bank ascribes to the business. If the market sector is highly volatile, it will be seen as having a high industry risk. Consequently, a bank will want minimal trading and financial risk associated with the project.

Financial risk

This is an assessment of the financial performance of the **8.17** business both past and future. It consists of an examination of the trading history and an explanation of any future changes or improvements in the business's performance.

Ratio analyses commonly used by banks

8.18 Banks will apply ratios to accounts to assist in the monitoring of performance of the business. A few of the most commonly used ratios are listed below, but this should not be taken as an exhaustive list.

Gearing or debt to equity ratio

8.19 This is defined as "all loans or debt (excluding hire-purchase and leasing) divided by the capital and reserves of the business (excluding goodwill and revaluation reserves)".

8.20 Traditionally this ratio should be approximately 0.5 on an ongoing basis; that is, the borrowing of the business should be less or equal to half of its capital. The maximum acceptable for a short-term period is normally 1. The ratio can also be expressed as a percentage, for example, 50 per cent or 100 per cent gearing.

Interest cover

8.21 This is defined as "profit before interest and tax divided by interest paid".

8.22 Normally the minimum acceptable ratio should be in the order of 3. The minimum acceptable after a large capital spend would be 2. This ratio gives an indication of the susceptibility of the business to an increase in interest rates or a decrease in profitability. The higher the ratio the more robust the business.

Debtor days

8.23 This is defined as "year end trade debtors divided by the total sales for the year, multiplied by 365".

8.24 Ideally this ratio would be expected to match the credit terms offered to the customers, *e.g.* 30 days. In practice, the longer the credit terms offered by the business, the lower the variance over these that the bank is likely to be comfortable with. Equally, the longer the debtor days are allowed to extend, the greater the likelihood that this may be seen as evidence of poor credit control, which increases the risk to the bank.

Creditor days

This is defined as "year end trade creditors divided by the total cost of sales for the year, multiplied by 365". **8.25**

This ratio should reflect average credit terms taken by the business. Ideally this ratio should be equal to the debtor days ratio for the business. If the creditor days are much lower than the debtor days, then this may reflect poor credit control or that the business is offering longer credit terms than the norm to win orders. Consequently the bank would be likely to request action to bring these back into balance. **8.26**

Stock turnover

This is defined as "total cost of sales for the year divided by year end stock". **8.27**

A stock turnover level of 5 or less would be considered low; however, much depends on the nature of the business. A business supplying perishable food products for the high street market would expect a very high stock turnover as there would be little or no finished goods stock. On the other hand, a jewellers business would expect a very low stock turnover ratio. **8.28**

Business medium and bank security

The nature of the business will be taken into account by banks when considering security. Different forms of business carry varying implications for their owners and it is important that owners understand the different levels of risk attaching to the different forms of business. **8.29**

Sole trader

Any person in business on his own account will be deemed a sole trader. A sole trader has no means of differentiating between business and personal assets. Therefore, if the business fails then all the personal assets of the sole trader are available for settlement of business debts.

Partnership

8.30 A partnership is a business venture of two or more people and is usually governed by a formal partnership agreement. If not, it is governed by one of the Partnership Acts. Each individual partner becomes liable for the whole debts of the partnership and not just for his share of them. This means that any person who is owed money by the partnership, or who wishes to sue a partnership for damages, can sue either any individual partner or partners or alternatively the whole partnership. An individual partner does have the right to reclaim the share due by the other partners of a successful claim made against him. If a partnership fails, then the partnership assets are used first to settle any debts. Thereafter, the personal estates of each of the partners can be used to settle any remaining debts. Therefore, all personal as well as business assets would be available for satisfaction of the debts of the business.

A limited company

8.31 A limited company is a separate legal entity from its shareholders. The only liability which shareholders have for the debts of a limited company is the nominal value of the shares owned by them.

8.32 What forms of security may a bank be looking for?

(a) *Personal guarantees* In a limited company the bank will frequently seek a personal guarantee from the directors or a third party. This will effectively remove the benefit of limited liability status. The greater the risk the bank perceive to a project, the larger the proportion of that debt that they are likely to seek as a personal guarantee.

(b) *Floating charges* A floating charge can only be taken over the assets of a limited company and increases the security by including such items as stock and debtors.

(c) *Standard security* A standard security is a legal charge over specific land and buildings owned by a business or a person and ensures that any proceeds from the sale of the land or buildings secured are first used to settle the amount due to the holder of the security.

Banks have to be extremely careful, however, because the value of assets of a business can be eroded as shown in Figure 8.2.   **8.33**

FIGURE 8.2

Value

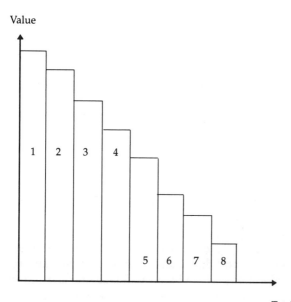

Total assets

Key

1 apparent balance sheet value of assets
2 deduct value of leased assets
3 deduct value of hire-purchase assets
4 deduct value of items subject to retention of title
5 apply discount for realisation of stock
6 apply discount for realisation of debtors
7 sums due to preferential creditors
8 apply discount for buildings, dilapidation,
      costs of sale, etc.

8.34   In this example the business has a balance sheet which seems to have plenty of asset cover for the bank. Unfortunately, if anything goes wrong then asset value can quickly diminish. First, the balance sheet contains leases at full value which are not owned by the business. Therefore, the bank cannot get any value from them; similarly with any assets which are subject to hire-purchase, so these too must be discounted.

8.35   Next the stock will contain items which are subject to retention of title and these, too, must be discounted. If the business ceases trading then work in progress will be of little or no value, so this must be discounted as well. It is notoriously difficult to collect debts when a company has ceased trading. It is therefore unlikely that the bank will be able to get full value for these, so they must also be discounted. Preferential creditors must be paid before the bank and therefore a further discount is required. Finally, as the company has been in trouble for some time, it is likely that the buildings have been neglected, so these will require to be discounted too.

8.36   It is easy to see, therefore, how an apparently strong balance sheet with lots of assets can quickly be eroded. It is for this reason that banks will heavily discount the amount they are prepared to lend against the face value of assets.

8.37   The development of a good working relationship between family businesses and their bankers and an understanding of the considerations which banks will take into account in deciding whether or not to assist a business is extremely important to the success of any family business.

CHAPTER 9

THE FISCAL DIMENSION

In any succession plan, the impact of taxation can materially **9.1** affect the outcome. Legal matters of this sort are subject to constant revision and change which can take place either by the passing of a Finance Act by Parliament, or by a ruling laid down in the Courts. It is therefore of great importance that plans are reviewed regularly to take account of such change.

Good fiscal planning requires, at the outset, a clear statement **9.2** of the objectives of the individual. These objectives can be stated in broad terms and are likely to be adapted as circumstances change. The establishment of objectives does, however, provide a mechanism which permits progress to be measured relative to the attainment of the objectives.

Planning of the financial affairs of individuals must, however, **9.3** also take account of the personal preferences of individuals in respect of matters such as risk profile and the nature of any investment offered to them.

ESTABLISHING INDEPENDENCE

Extracting income

During the business life, both owner managers and **9.4** shareholders extract income from the business. The way in which income is extracted and the associated tax costs will be directly related to the form of the business entity.

Sole traders and partners will pay income tax on the full **9.5** amount of the profits assessable in the fiscal year. The change in 1996/97 to current year basis of assessment means that the profits assessed in any fiscal year are those earned in the financial year ending within the fiscal year. A fiscal year runs from April 6 in any year to April 5 in the following year. Funds retained within the business and reflected in the capital and current accounts are likely to represent substantially earnings which have been taxed and not withdrawn from the business or capital introduced from other sources.

9.6 When a business is expanding and there is an increasing requirement for working capital, it may be beneficial to contrast the position of the sole trader or partner with that of the company. It must, however, be recognised that tax is only one of a large number of factors to be considered when selecting the most appropriate form of vehicle for a business.

9.7 A company pays corporation tax at rates which are currently lower than the top rate of income tax. The owner manager is subject to income tax under the PAYE system on the salary and benefits which he receives from the business. Thus the facility exists to retain funds within the business more tax efficiently. It must, however, be recognised that a further charge to income tax is likely to arise when and if these retained funds are subsequently distributed and a charge to capital gains tax is likely to arise if the shares are transferred or sold.

9.8 Succession planning is, to a large extent, recognising certain events which will happen in the future, and planning for these events. Figure 9.1 is a simple illustration of the way in which assets are generated during a business life. The business, in many cases an asset itself, is the engine which generates the funds to help establish assets either in the form of a pension fund or in the form of personal assets. This is true whether or not the business is incorporated.

9.9 The future event which is certain to happen is the planned succession of the business. The succession will be more easily achieved if the incumbent has attained financial independence from the business by the establishment of a pension fund and a personal asset base.

FIGURE 9.1

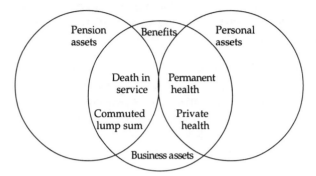

This independence can best be achieved by careful planning **9.10** over a number of years, taking account of the ability of the business to generate the cash necessary to permit the extraction of funds. The long-term extraction of funds should be an integral part of the business plan and the cash flow projections. Sole traders and partners, in addition to normal drawings, have the ability to draw additional lump sums from time to time. In addition to salary and benefits, profits can be extracted from a company over a number of years by voting bonuses or declaring dividends. Lump sums received in this way are generally treated differently from salary which is used to meet day-to-day living expenses. In both cases such sums, properly invested, can provide flexibility when planning, both in respect of future income and capital.

At this point the need for long-term planning becomes **9.11** evident. Each individual must set his own objectives and seek to invest sums in such a way as to meet these objectives. Some may prefer greater emphasis on pension funding. In other cases circumstances may dictate differently. The point is that, either way, there exists a point of reference against which to measure progress.

Pension planning itself is far from simple and specialist **9.12** advice should be sought. Two principal types of pension arrangement are in existence. Personal pension plans can be taken out by the self-employed and those not in pensionable employment. Executive pension plans can be taken out by companies on behalf of senior executives who work in the company.

9.13 In normal circumstances both the individual paying contributions to a personal pension plan and the company paying contributions to an executive pension plan, will obtain tax relief on the premiums paid. The premiums themselves are invested in what presently amounts to a fund which grows free of tax. This environment should have a considerable effect on the growth of pension funds where premiums are invested regularly over an extended period.

9.14 Pension schemes can assist the planning process in two other ways. First, they can provide life assurance cover in the event of the unexpected death of the member. This policy can be written in trust for the benefit of dependents and can therefore avoid aggregation with the estate of the deceased for inheritance tax purposes. Secondly, on retiral, the member can opt to exchange part of his pension fund for a lump sum. The level of the lump sum is dependent on the type of pension scheme in place.

9.15 It must be recognised, however, that the level of pension provision is linked directly to the earnings of the individual and provision may be further restricted by legislation. Dividends paid by companies are not classed as emoluments and cannot therefore be taken into account when assessing pension entitlement. Emoluments consist of salary, bonus and benefits in kind.

9.16 Careful consideration has therefore to be given to the net cost of extracting income from a company. Salary and bonus carry a charge to national insurance for both the employer and employee. While the charge payable by the employee is currently capped at an overall maximum there is no such ceiling on the contribution paid by the employer.

9.17 A dividend, however, has currently to be accompanied by a remittance of advance corporation tax to the Collector of

Taxes. Although this is recoverable against the company's mainstream corporation tax charge, care has to be taken regarding timing as cash flow will be affected. It is therefore important that the reason for extracting income is understood and the cost attaching to the alternative methods are compared. The ACT regime will, however, be abolished from April 1999.

When preparing for retirement the incumbent must recognise **9.18** the additional cost of expenditure which may previously have been met by the business. Notwithstanding that income tax was previously paid on such items, he may have to fully fund a car in future. The telephone bill and private health care may also have to be funded. It should also be recognised that, on retirement, the death in service element of pension provision will no longer exist. It may therefore be necessary to consider additional life cover at this time.

Extracting capital

Where insufficient funds have been extracted by the **9.19** incumbent prior to the intended date for retirement, it may be necessary to generate a lump sum from the business prior to passing it on to the next generation. In a company this could be achieved by:

(a)   purchase of own shares by the company;
(b)   sale of shares.

In a sole trade or partnership it could be achieved by withdrawing capital, whether or not accompanied by a revaluation of chargeable assets.

Purchase of own shares

Since 1982, a company has been permitted to purchase its **9.20** own shares providing certain legal conditions are met. Tax legislation, however, draws a further distinction and lays down detailed rules which have to be met if the buy back is to be referred to as a qualifying distribution. If the detailed conditions are not met the transaction is classified as a non-qualifying distribution.

9.21 It is of vital importance to ensure that the full consequences of a company purchasing its own shares are understood before the transaction is undertaken and to assist in this process the Inland Revenue will advise, in advance, of their view of the proposed transaction. The nature of the distribution can have differing consequences for the company which can affect cash flow and future distribution policies. As a result of the buy back the ownership percentages of other shareholders are changed.

9.22 The consequence for the vendor is, however, of equal importance. A qualifying buy back is treated as a capital receipt in the hands of the recipient. A non-qualifying buy back will be treated as income. The former will therefore be subject to capital gains tax while the latter will be subject to income tax.

9.23 Whether or not it is possible to structure the transaction to best suit the needs of the vendor will depend on individual circumstances.

Sale of shares

9.24 The sale of shares will give rise to a capital receipt in the hands of the vendor. Normally, a sale to an independent party will be accepted as being at full value. Where, however, sales take place between family members, legislation permits the Inland Revenue to substitute market value for the consideration paid if they consider that the asset was undervalued on transfer.

Capital taxes

9.25 Income taxes are generally well understood but capital taxes can be encountered less frequently. There are two main taxes which have to be considered by the family when considering succession planning. These are:

    (a) capital gains tax;
    (b) inheritance tax.

9.26 These taxes are complex and the following is intended to do no more than highlight some features of the legislation.

Professional advice must be obtained to ensure that proposed transactions are properly structured and will have the anticipated result agreed with the Inland Revenue.

Successive governments in recent years have recognised the importance of an enterprise culture and have sought to encourage it by the enhancement of existing reliefs and the introduction of new reliefs within fiscal legislation. These reliefs, as they apply to family companies, will be mentioned in the following paragraphs.   **9.27**

Capital gains tax

Capital gains tax charges tax on any capital gains realised from the sale of assets. The tax charge is levied in respect of that fiscal year and the rate of tax is the rate payable if the gain was assumed to be the top slice of income received by the tax payer in that fiscal year. The rate at which capital gains tax is payable is therefore equivalent to the income tax rates in any year.   **9.28**

Gains can arise on the disposal of chargeable assets whether by gift or sale. If assets are transferred to family members, it is almost certain that they will be held as connected persons within the capital gains tax legislation and market value will be used to calculate the 'gain' arising on the transfer of the asset.   **9.29**

When computing any gain, the cost of the asset is increased by indexation allowance which adjusts the historical cost of the asset, or its value at March 1982, for the effect of inflation in the period to April 1998. The intention of the indexation allowance is to assess to tax real gains rather than inflationary gains. Following April 1998 the cost of the asset will no longer be indexed. Instead, the gain chargeable to tax will be reduced in respect of the period for which the asset has been held after April 1998. This reduction, called taper relief, will be greater for business assets, thus maintaining focus on the enterprise culture.   **9.30**

Legislation allows inter-spouse transfers to be made on the basis that neither gain nor loss arises on the transfer. This   **9.31** can be a valuable relief when planning family finances but it must be recognised that inter-spouse gifts should be outright gifts with no arrangement for the eventual return to the donor spouse of any proceeds from a subsequent sale of the asset.

9.32 Another important measure is retirement relief. This relief, given as a sliding scale which is dependent upon the length of the period of ownership of the business, can result in either a direct tax saving on the sale of shares if shares are sold or an uplift in the base cost of shares if they are gifted.

9.33 Provisions extend to sole traders and partners and retirement relief may be available when an interest in such an entity is gifted or sold. Care has to be taken, however, to ensure that what is disposed of is part of the business itself as opposed to an asset used for business purposes.

9.34 Retirement relief provisions have to be reviewed carefully to ensure that all qualifying conditions are met at the time of gift and that the relief is maximised. Care has also to be taken to ensure that the effects of the interaction of retirement relief with other reliefs are fully understood in advance of the proposed gift.

9.35 Following the introduction of taper relief, retirement relief is to be gradually phased out over a five-year period. Those considering a transition within that timescale need to consider the implications of this in their plan.

9.36 When considering transfers of assets, consideration could be given to examining the terms of hold over relief. The effect of this legislation is to allow the donee to inherit the same base cost of the asset received for capital gains tax purposes as that of the donor. For the purposes of this legislation, shares in private family companies which carry on a trade are treated as business assets.

9.37 The terms of the legislation require careful study and care has to be taken to ensure that the relief is not restricted or that the effects of such restrictions are known in advance of the transfer.

No charge to capital gains tax arises on death and the **9.38** beneficiaries inherit assets from the estate of the deceased at full market value. Effectively any gains tax charge is washed out of the assets on death.

Inheritance tax

To compensate for the lack of a charge to capital gains tax, **9.39** inheritance tax is applied on death. It is also chargeable on a lifetime transfer into a discretionary trust.

No tax is payable on the first £223,000 of value transferred at **9.40** present but this level of exempt transfers will vary with changing legislation. Thereafter tax is levied on chargeable transfers at the rate of 40 per cent on death and 20 per cent in respect of chargeable lifetime transfers.

Inheritance tax has been the subject of much criticism as it **9.41** has been classified as a tax avoidable by those who can afford to plan to minimise its impact through the use of reliefs such as potentially exempt transfers and business property relief.

The importance of these reliefs—and in particular business **9.42** property relief—to the family business cannot, however, be overstated and the need to ensure legislation which facilitates the transmission of enterprise is vital for this huge sector of the economy.

Structuring the estate

From the above, it can be seen that the entire family should **9.43** consider their respective objectives to ensure the optimum utilisation of the allowances and reliefs available within the tax system.

For example, shares left to a spouse may then be sold by her, **9.44** thereby converting an asset which qualified for business property relief to an asset which will not. In this way, the exposure of the family estate to tax on the demise of the surviving spouse has been increased. Better planning may have allowed such a position to have been avoided.

9.45 A common problem faced in such planning can be to establish who should hold the family company shares. Within the family system there may be many good reasons why shares should not be passed outright to the next generation or indeed to a spouse. An interim vehicle can therefore be sought and this vehicle can take the form of a trust. There are three main and distinct forms of trust which can be considered:

      (a) a trust where the beneficiary has an interest in possession;
      (b) an accumulation and maintenance trust;
      (c) a discretionary trust.

9.46 The use of trusts therefore allows value to pass out of the estate of the donor and future growth in value of shares passed in this way does not enhance the value of the donor's estate.

9.47 The price to be paid by the donor for his altruism is that ownership and control of these shares passes to trustees and, while in certain circumstances the donor (or settler) may be a trustee, he cannot control the shares in the same way as before. Trustees have a statutory duty to act in the best interests of the beneficiaries of the trust. Acting in this manner may not always coincide with the wishes of the settler. The types of trust can be explained as follows.

Interest in possession

9.48 This trust exists where one or more beneficiaries have an absolute right to the income of the trust, either during their lifetime or for a fixed period.

Accumulation and maintenance

9.49 This type of trust is given favourable treatment by the inheritance tax legislation and is established generally to benefit minor children who must be granted a right to income by the age of 25.

Discretionary trust

The trustees of a discretionary trust generally have the right **9.50** to decide whether and when to distribute income or capital within the named class of beneficiary.

The treatment of the above trusts varies within fiscal **9.51** legislation and the rates of tax payable on income can also vary. It is therefore vital to be clear as to the objectives which the trust has to fulfil in the succession strategy before any transfer is made and for proper professional advice to be taken.

So why plan?

The family can often seem to be beset by formidable obstacles **9.52** which are unfamiliar to them, faced with issues relative to:

(a) decisions within the family system;
(b) projections about retirement;
(c) the structure of transfers;
(d) the value of transfers;
(e) the fiscal consequences of transfers.

The donor may well seek solace through inaction. It can, after **9.53** all, be argued that with no capital gains tax on death, the donor can avoid some of the fiscal and valuation issues he would otherwise face. He may take the view that any charge to inheritance tax could be met by the beneficiaries or covered by an appropriate life assurance policy.

It is to be hoped, however, that the problems which can arise **9.54** from succumbing to inaction in succession planning are now only too clear.

CHAPTER 10

A CASE STUDY

Note: This case has been prepared for training purposes only and not to illustrate either effective or ineffective handling of an administrative situation. I would like to take this opportunity to thank the family involved for providing permission for me to use their story.

This case study has been prepared to illustrate and reinforce a lot of the points made in previous chapters. It clearly shows how complicated and messy it can turn out for future generations when the consequences of decisions which were implemented during family business transitions were not anticipated. This is a live, Scottish family business case study: the names have been changed to ensure confidentiality. Fortunately, the family concerned was able, with help, to find a way out of the mess in which they found themselves, and today the family business is successful and thriving—but only after a heavy price was paid in terms of the family's health and relationships.

This case will take you through a multigenerational family tree (called a genogram) over four generations and 100 years of family business decisions. There are four critical junctures at which major decisions were taken by the family, and after which the ramifications of these decisions were "lived out" with considerable difficulty by the next generation.

Please use each of the critical junctures in the case—the transition times—to think through the issues identified in earlier chapters and to come up with your own ideas about the advantages and disadvantages of each option. This is an excellent way to check your understanding of the issues and dilemmas facing families in business. A list of options for each of the junctures is provided at the end of the case for you to check your own ideas. There are no right or wrong answers—only options and consequences. The hope is that the case study will illustrate that it is the responsibility of business-owning families to work out, in advance, the consequences of their own intentions and to communicate these openly.

The earlier chapters and this case study can leave no one in any doubt about the need for families in business to surround themselves with a support team covering the expertise required to predict and prevent the unwanted consequences imposed on families and businesses of the important decisions being made at transition times. Unfortunately, the research cited throughout this book has shown that families prefer to "do-it-themselves". This case study shows what can happen under these conditions.

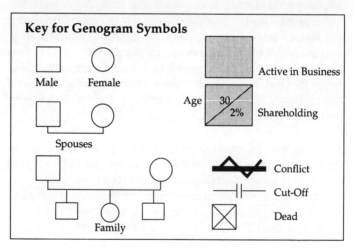

STEWART CLARK ENGINEERING (SCOTLAND) LTD

PART 1

In 1996, Stewart Clark Engineering (Scotland) Ltd is an example of a company whose performance is the envy of its industrial competitors. The firm imports electrical components, adds value to them and sells them on to its large customer base in Scotland. It has a net worth of £1 million, is significantly more profitable than its competitors and, with a century of business experience under its belt, has a name and reputation which is not only the envy of others in the trade, but is also apparently the name that most customers "want to do business with". But the favourable circumstances enjoyed by the present Stewart Clark (fourth generation) and his relatives might never have come about, as a brief tour of the history of this family business clearly shows.

Established in 1902, the first Stewart Clark saw an opening in the supply of mechanical handling gear and set up a small engineering company in Caithness in the very north of Scotland. He was aged 32 when the firm started, and was married with four children, all under the age of seven. His six employees manufactured jigs and hoists while he travelled extensively to source raw materials of the right quality, and to negotiate deals with attractive margins with his customers. The business grew steadily and within the next 20 years his three sons joined the business. The family worked together for the next eight years and Stewart began planning the transfer of ownership and control to the next generation (see Figure 10.1).

FIGURE 10.1: The Clark Family in 1930

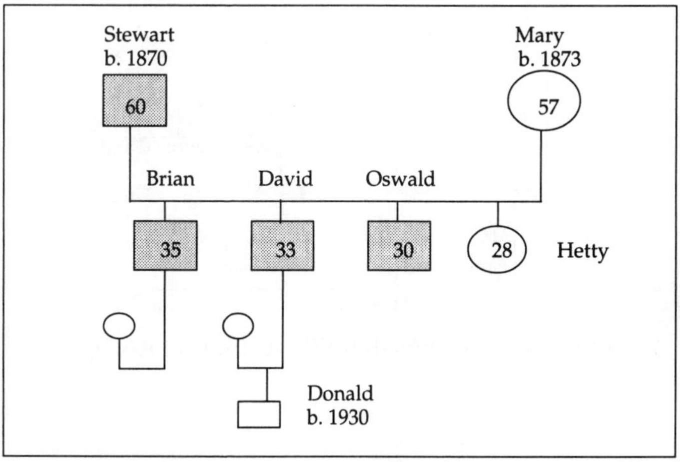

The first transition is completed. What are the implications of this decision?

The first critical juncture

Put yourself in Stewart's shoes and list his options for transferring ownership to the next generation. Then, list the advantages and drawbacks of each of the main options (see Appendix I).

PART 2

Stewart and his wife Mary both felt strongly that they wanted all of their children to benefit as equally as was possible from the available wealth which could be passed on to them. To keep all the offspring equal, he gifted 45 per cent of the shares to the boys (each receiving 15 per cent) over the five years leading up to his retirement, and on his death, transferred the remainder via a trust to Mary and on her death to his daughter Hetty. Hetty did not work in the business (Figure 10.2).

FIGURE 10.2: After the first transition

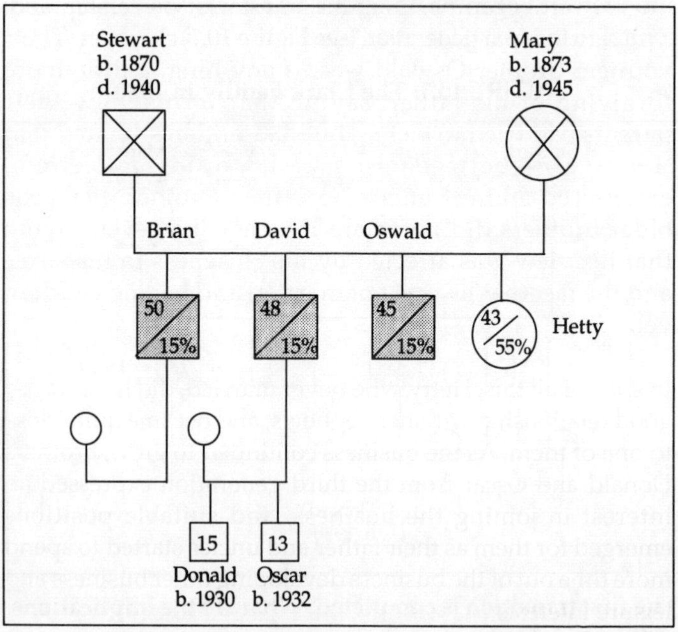

PART 3

Stewart explained to Mary that it was his wish to divide the total spoils equally. He therefore set things up so that Hetty could live off the dividends generated by the business, and for the boys to live off their salaries augmented by their share of the dividends. This, he thought, would bring equal incomes for all so that they all benefited from their parents' work and sacrifices equally.

Unfortunately for Stewart and Mary, things did not work out the way they wanted them to. After the death of their mother, when the inheritance was finalised, the brothers were disgusted that their sister effectively had control of the business, especially since she did not work in the business. In addition they did not want to have her working there. They felt that the net result of all their work over the years was a comfortable life for their little sister. They felt that their father had let them down.

The two elder brothers, Brian and David, were extremely disgruntled, particularly David as he had children. Their younger brother Oswald was, if anything, a little more forgiving of his father, saying that in his view their parents had tried to be fair, but had underestimated that the rivalry between them all would make them embittered and estranged once their mother died. His older brothers did not share his view, however, saying that his view was affected by his closeness to his sister and the fact that he was not married and had no children yet.

In spite of all this, Hetty, who never married, did have a very good relationship with her nephews, and became quite close to one of them. As the business continued to grow, brothers Donald and Oscar from the third generation expressed an interest in joining the business, and suitable positions emerged for them as their father and uncles started to spend more time out of the business developing other business and leisure interests.

The second critical juncture approaches

What do you think will happen to the ownership of the business at this second transition? Explore the options and consequences (see Appendix II for some options).

What issues should these second generation family members be aware of as they start to consider their retirement? (Chapter 4)

What other issues are emerging which are specific to family-run businesses?

Figure 10.3 shows what happened to the ownership of the business. The three brothers decided to consolidate their ownership and divide it equally between their sons/ nephews. By 1965, Donald and Oscar both owned 22.5 per cent each. As time went on, these brothers got on reasonably

FIGURE 10.3: Preparing for the second transition

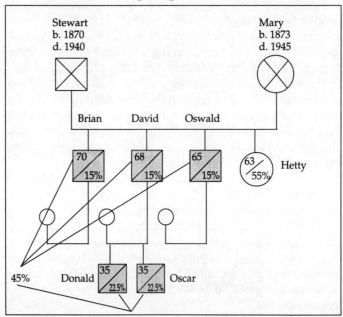

well, with occasional rivalries taking up some of their time. Fortunately, the ruffled feathers were usually smoothed over without any loss of face on either side.

Then Aunt Hetty's bombshell hit the family (Figure 10.4) and set in place a very intense rivalry from which there was to be no recovery. Brothers Donald and Oscar had never actually discussed it, but each had hoped and expected Hetty to divide her shares equally between them, following her father's attempt at equality. However, her leaving all the shares to Donald surprised everyone (including Donald) and caused an immediate rift between the two brothers. In fact, each refused to speak to the other from that point onward.

This made life very uncomfortable for everyone in the family business system. Cousins and in-laws ceased to communicate, and the non-family managers in the business were made to feel their allegiance could only be with one of the two brothers. It even had ramifications beyond the normal

FIGURE 10.4: The Clark Family in 1970

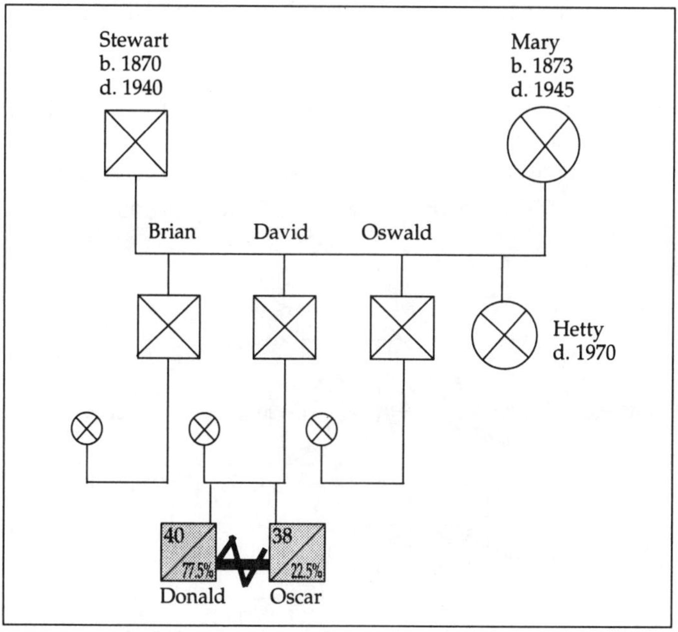

operations of the business. Executive decisions could only be taken at the meetings held by the company accountant, who travelled monthly to the firm and, acting as the communications conduit, passed notes from one brother to the other, avoiding (where possible) the punches and blows which were thrown as he separated the sparring brothers.

In 1982, divine intervention took over, and Donald died of cancer at age 52, six months after the diagnosis. This precipitated a crisis not only for the surviving brother, but also for his widow Susan, who found herself in a state of shock and grief; she also became the majority shareholder in a business in which she had never worked. It was her view that the business had torn her family apart and led her husband to an early grave. She and her daughter were left wondering how on earth this had all come about, and what they ought to do next.

Susan was 15 years younger than her husband. Oscar became worried about the prospect of her re-marrying and the potential impact of a second husband on the business and on his own position. He and his accountant also discussed their concerns about her ability to spend significant amounts of money with great relish and speed. Figure 10.5 shows the situation in 1982.

PART 4

Even when he was ill, Donald had not given any indication of his plans for succession in the business. His daughter was not interested in the business (for which he had been grateful

FIGURE 10.5: The Clark Family in 1982

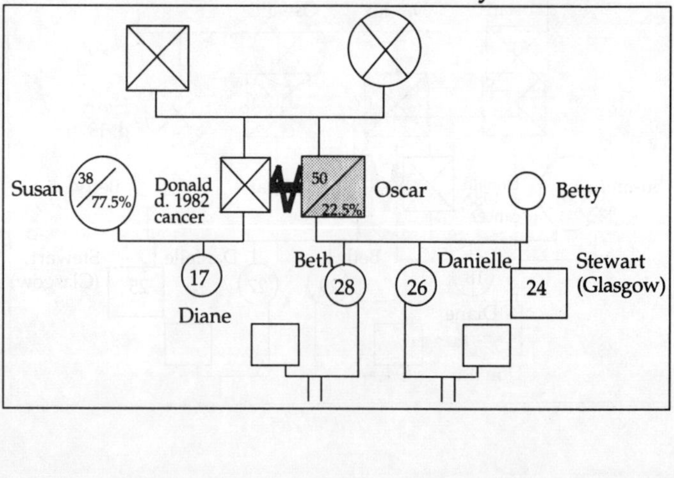

as he dearly wanted to keep her out of the fracas). However, he had said to his wife that with every day that went by, his brother Oscar became more embittered that the success of the business was in his view adding to his niece's wealth.

Donald's widow inherited the shares at this third stage of the critical juncture; and all the angst that went with them. Oscar found himself in an intolerable position and decided to seek advice about his situation. He had no intention of adding more value to the family business when his family were merely the minority beneficiaries. For him, this juncture was unfinished business. He became very agitated about the shares, and pressed very hard to find a way to buy them back from Susan.

At this third critical juncture, explore the options for the individuals concerned, for each of the family branches and for the business

(a) If you are Oscar, what are your options? (see Appendix III for some options)

(b) If you are Susan, what are your options? (see Appendix IV for some options)

(c) If you are Stewart, what must you consider? (see Chapter 5)

(d) If you were the business, what would your key concerns be, and what protection would you want from the family feud?

Figure 10.6 shows what happened at the third critical juncture.

FIGURE 10.6: The Clark Family in 1983

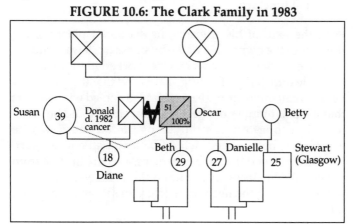

Oscar bought the shares from his sister-in-law and for the first time had total ownership and control of the company. Susan was paid an amount for the shares and received a pension from the company.

However, Oscar was still unhappy with his situation and started thinking ahead to the next critical juncture. He then decided to initiate his own succession planning. Now 51, he had a son in Glasgow studying to be a CA. His daughters were married, and none showed any inclination to join the firm. He initiated a conversation with Stewart explaining that if he were to consider returning North to join the family business, then he (Oscar) would work out a plan handing over the business to him with no future interference (Chapter 4).

Stewart felt that having worked with an accounting practice for two years, he was now ready to apply his skills in the management of a real company, rather than the numbers representing the firms of his clients. Oscar was delighted to see Stewart join the business, but was determined that Stewart and his sisters, Beth and Danielle, should never experience what he had seen take place amongst his own generation, and amongst his father's generation.

The final juncture

With the help of his advisers, he set about planning the transfer of the ownership of the business to Stewart and his sisters, ensuring that Stewart, who worked in the business, had a clear majority of voting shares and that the daughters held a small minority of shares. He also agreed with Stewart that a small number of shares (5 per cent) should be given to Bill, a long-term employee of the business, whose experience, both agreed, would be invaluable to Stewart. He then followed this up by ensuring a secure income from outside the business so that he could let Stewart take over without feeling the need to interfere to safeguard his own interest.

This took a lot of planning. The accountant's task was to get Oscar out of the business and to set up the structure of the company to allow Stewart the independence he required. He also had to ensure that the daughters received equal shares of their parents' estates. This was done by ensuring that in their wills the parents left other assets including the family home to the daughters to equalise the position.

For Stewart, the concentration of the shares back into the hands of the owner manager was a key issue and was a precondition of his taking over the firm. He and his father reflected upon how complicated it had all become as events had unfolded over the years (Figure 10.7).

The fourth critical juncture

How did this family end up in such a mess?

What lessons can other family firms learn from their experiences?

What specific issues must advisers take into account when dealing with family business clients?

FIGURE 10.7: The Clark Family Business Shareholding in 1991

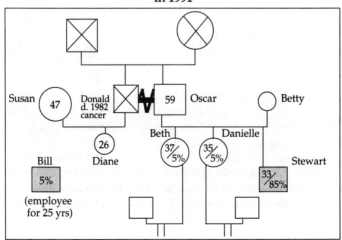

This case presents the reader with the opportunity to apply the required thought processes at each critical juncture and to anticipate consequences. It also allows us to reflect on the types of issues which are universally seen in families who own businesses.

1 Family values and norms

All families have rules and norms which guide their actions. Unfortunately, these are usually unspoken and so are likely to cause difficulties for those who are affected by them. In this case, the following unspoken values or norms existed:

(i) "children should inherit equally the assets available": Stewart and Mary's wish to equally distribute their assets amongst the four offspring led to disruption which was carried forward in the next two generations.

However, "equal" did not turn out to be "equitable" because an inactive owner controlled the business and active family members were left to run the business and create wealth for the inactive owner to enjoy. This outcome was a surprise to those who inherited it.

Oscar learned the hard way that other approaches to the distribution of assets must be considered when a business is involved. He learned that in his family, ownership and management had been separated but the active owners were unable to control the business without deferring managerial decisions to inactive owners. While this may work in some families, it did not fit with his own family's relationship dynamics.

(ii) "we do not communicate our intentions to our children": Stewart and Mary, in their efforts to keep their children equally provided for, apparently did not discuss their plans with them. Likewise, Hetty's will was a "bombshell" for her nephews, who were expecting to receive the rest of the shares equally, as their father and uncles had arranged in accordance with the family tradition. Note also that Donald's death revealed that he had not communicated any plans despite the emerging need to clarify the future of the business.

When a business will be affected by the disposal of an estate, as in the case of a family business, the intentions of the senior generation must be known in advance: specifically what will happen to the ownership of the business, and how the future leadership of the firm will be decided. This way, the business will be protected in the event of a sudden death or incapacity, and there will be no surprises that may cause family rifts.

Again, Oscar learned from the previous generations that it was better to communicate his intentions well in advance and to ensure that offspring understand how their needs and those of the business are being taken care of.

2 Structure policies before the need

The Clark family struggled over the generations with ownership issues (trying to prevent dilution of the shares if Susan re-married for example) and management issues (working in conflictive conditions).

Families in business usually have some difficulty separating their roles as shareholders from their roles as managers and from their roles in the family. This can often lead to difficulties around who gets jobs in the firm, and who gets to own shares in the firm. All families need to have policies for entry into and exit from the family business, both for ownership (who gets shares?, what type?, who doesn't?, on what basis?) and for management (who gets a job?, who doesn't?, on what basis?, how do we get rid of them?).

Again, Oscar's view was that the firm's shareholding needed to be protected from potential dilution and the threat of unwanted owners, and to again ensure that active owners could be in control of the business. All family businesses are likely to face these issues as families grow and tend to take up managerial positions in the firm, so all family businesses need policies in advance of the need to address them. All families in business should seek help with the creation of their family constitution, in which these policies reside. The contents of a family constitution depend on the individual wants and dynamics of each family.

3 Communication, communication, communication

As can be seen above, family members often do not communicate their intentions to each other. Any policies (formal or informal) must be communicated to family members in order to be effective.

Families need to have a forum for discussing the business of the family (a "family council") and a forum for discussing the business of the business (a board of directors or an advisory board). The board of directors will be more effective when it knows the wishes of its owner-shareholders. When the directors and the shareholders are the same people, they should create a family council to establish their guiding values, norms and policies and communicate these to other members of the family who may aspire to join the firm or to own it some day. This will also clarify matters for non-family managers.

4 Get the best professional advice the firm can afford— and involve the family

Despite taking advice to ensure an equal inheritance for his offspring, Stewart Sr. will most likely be looking down at the result and be very dissatisfied with the outcome.

The traditional approach to professional advice is that the client is the senior generation family member who owns the majority of the shares. This person then separately gets advice from legal, banking and accounting people, then decides a course of action. Leaving out the rest of the family is dangerous—this "DIY" approach leads to surprises and unwanted consequences. The aspirations and expectations of others must be taken into account before a final course of action can be decided upon.

Family firms can and do work spectacularly well—but the issues above have to be predicted, and their consequences planned for and communicated. The onus is on the family to use their advisers wisely, to communicate their intentions to each other, to seek help to ensure that the consequences of decisions being made have been thought through in advance, and to re-visit these issues at least once a year.

APPENDIX I

The First Juncture: Assessing the Options in 1930

Options	Advantages	Disadvantages
1. "Active owners equal" All the shares in the business are transferred to his sons equally on his death or during his lifetime.	(a) The business is controlled by those who work within it and as all receive the same number of shares there should be no friction caused, if they are able to achieve consensus.	(a) Should a transfer occur during Stewart's lifetime, he may not have sufficient income outwith the business to live on.
		(b) Should a transfer occur at his death, what will his widow live on?
		(c) In either case, will there be sufficient other capital to ensure that his daughter receives the same value as her inheritance as her three brothers?
		(d) No one brother will be seen as the man in charge as there is no differentiation in the shareholdings.

Options	Advantages	Disadvantages
2. "Active owners with nominated leader" All the shares in the business are transferred to his sons but one son is seen as key to the success of the business and he receives more shares than his two brothers.	(a) As in Option 1, with the additional plus point that one of the sons is established as the key director.	(a) As in Option 1, with the additional potential disadvantage that disharmony is caused between the three brothers.
3. "All children equal" Shares in the business are transferred equally to all children either during his lifetime or on Stewart's death.	(a) This may seem to be the fairest solution, as all children are participating equally.	(a) The problems of living expenses either during his lifetime or on his death are still there for Stewart and his wife.
		(b) Shares in the business are going to someone who is not actively involved in the business, namely the daughter. In addition, if she marries her husband would gain an interest in the business through her. This may not be suitable.

Options	Advantages	Disadvantages
"Keeping everyone involved" Majority of the shares transferred to the sons with a small holding being transferred to the daughter, either during his lifetime or on his death.	(a) A large majority of the shares would be controlled by those working within the business ("active owners"). (b) Daughter ("inactive owner") would still have a modest interest in the business but would effectively have no power.	(a) The same disadvantages as previously in relation to living expenses for Stewart and his wife. (b) Would there be sufficient funds in the rest of Stewart's estate to equalise the position in relation to his daughter? If not, disharmony amongst the family could result.
5. "Procrastination" Retain all the shares until his death and then transfer them to his wife.	(a) His wife would be guaranteed an income following Stewart's death.	(a) The problem of transference to the next generation is merely delayed. (b) The sons who are working in the business will have no interest in the shares until the death of their mother.

Options	Advantages	Disadvantages
6. "Set up trust to separate capital and income" Retain the shares until his death and set up a trust, whereby the income goes to his wife on his death and the capital is then transferred to the children equally on his wife's death.	(a) He and his wife have an income during their lifetimes. (b) He can determine the quantum of shares going to each of his children on the death of his wife, so the succession is established.	(a) Although the succession is established, those working within the business do not have ownership until the death of their mother. If Stewart never gets round to deciding on the division of the wealth/shareholding/leadership questions, it can put the burden on Mary.
7. "The potentially equitable" option Reorganise the share capital and transfer ordinary voting shares to the sons and coupon shares with the restricted voting rights to the daughter and also possibly to the wife.	(a) Those working in the business have the voting control. (b) His daughter, and possibly his wife, as "inactive owners" are guaranteed an income stream without being able to interfere in the normal day-to-day business of the company.	(a) It would still be necessary to equalise the daughter's inheritance in view of the different values which would be placed on ordinary shares and coupon shares.

Options	Advantages	Disadvantages
8. "The potentially inequitable" option Transfer a minority of the shares equally to his sons in his lifetime and set up a trust for the benefit of his wife, with the capital going to his daughter on her death.	(a) The sons obtain an interest in the business in which they work. (b) Stewart retains an income stream during his lifetime. (c) Stewart's widow retains an income stream following his death. (d) His daughter has an income stream following her mother's death.	(a) The company is controlled by someone who is not actively involved in the business. (b) Should the daughter marry, control could pass to someone outwith the immediate family.
9. "Sell up" Sell the company.	(a) Stewart and his wife obtain capital which they can use to provide an income or partially transfer to the family.	(a) Their sons may lose their jobs.

APPENDIX II

OPTION 1   Sell the company. This may prove to be very attractive to Hetty and also to Brian and Oswald as they have no children of their own.

OPTION 2   Brian, David and Oswald set up liferent and fee trusts so that on their death income from dividends goes to their wives and on their death, shares are transferred to Donald and Oscar, hopefully equally. It would also be hoped that Hetty would leave her shares equally to Donald and Oscar.

OPTION 3   Brian, David and Oswald gift their shares equally to Donald and Oscar during their lifetime on the basis that Donald and Oscar are now working in the business. Hetty also gives her shares during her lifetime to Donald and Oscar equally, although this is possibly less likely in view of her requirement for an income flow and the fact that she has no pension because she did not work in the business.

OPTION 4   Brian, David and Oswald gift their shares equally during their lifetimes to Donald and Oscar. Hetty leaves her shares on her death to one of the brothers. This is the scenario most likely to create family problems, as it would give either Donald or Oscar total control over the company.

APPENDIX III

Oscar's options are extremely limited and these would appear to be as follows:

(a) buy out Susan;
(b) attempt to sell his share of the business;
(c) continue running the business under the control of Susan.

APPENDIX IV

The main options so far as Susan is concerned appear to be as follows:

(a) she sells her shares either to an outside party or to Oscar;

(b) she retains her shares and does not interfere in the day-to-day running of the business, but receives her dividends;

(c) she has herself appointed as a director of the company and receives a salary;

(d) she gets rid of Oscar and brings in other management.

INDEX

99